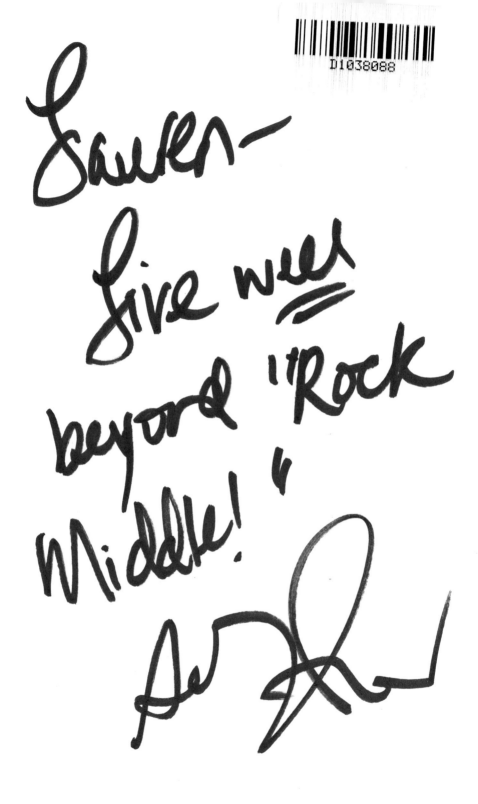

Lauren —

Live well
beyond "Rock
Middle! "

PRAISE FOR
HITTING ROCK MIDDLE

"In *Hitting Rock Middle*, Sallie Holder tackles an issue that can affect every one of us, no matter who you are or your stage in life—feeling stuck somewhere between 'rock bottom' and your greatest potential. Sallie's story, and the advice she offers within, can help anyone climb out of that place in the middle and reach new heights in life. An absolute must-read!"

—BUSY PHILIPPS

Actor and *New York Times* Bestselling Author of *This Will Only Hurt A Little*

"In *Hitting Rock Middle*, Sallie Holder deftly touches on a common thread affecting every one of us regardless of circumstance—getting stuck in a rut. Through her own experience, she provides a practical road map and workable strategy for dealing with the fear and growing pains that accompany change. In a society where women have been conditioned to feel they should come last, Sallie's reassurance offers unimaginable freedom to those who desire to put themselves first but don't know how. Her advice and steady guidance will enhance relationships with everyone in your life, including, most importantly, the relationship you have with yourself. If you do the work, the results are clear. Sallie's own story is proof."

—CAROLYN MANNO

TV Anchor and Reporter with CNN

"Most of us, if we're honest with ourselves, know exactly what it feels like to hit rock middle, and few of us know how or have the courage to climb out. Over the past ten years, I've watched Sallie Holder do just that; and now that she has found where she is meant to be, she has treated the rest of us to a road map and inspiration to live unique lives that are not only successful, but genuinely happy!

I've had the good fortune to watch thousands of women lift themselves up to happier places, but none has been more poignant or inspiring than Sallie. In *Hitting Rock Middle*, she not only tells her incredible story, but also both describes a condition most people experience and provides a path for each of us to thrive instead of just live. That makes this book a must-read!"

—MIKE LOHNER
Chairman, Stella & Dot Family of Brands

"By my midthirties I had everything the world measures as success, and yet I wanted out. In that moment I chose change. I decided that the risk of staying the same was far greater than the risk of change. Once I crossed that bridge, I started running toward the safety of joy. Sallie Holder did too. In *Hitting Rock Middle* she helps you find the road to the same bridge. She shares the wisdom of her own journey and that of the clients she has coached. I will state it emphatically: Seek joy!"

—RICHARD SHERIDAN
CEO, Chief Storyteller, Menlo Innovations
Author of *Joy, Inc: How We Built A Workplace People Love* and *Chief Joy Officer: How Great Leaders Elevate Human Energy and Eliminate Fear*

"This book is for every person who has sought happiness from success, only to realize the formula is flipped. By sharing her personal experience, Sallie drills down to one of the key problems facing so many of us: What do we do when we realize career success doesn't fulfill us in the way we anticipated? This book provides readers with the insight to begin to see their careers (and lives) from a new perspective."

KATE FAGAN
New York Times Bestselling Author of *What Made Maddie Run* and Former ESPN Anchor

AND

KATHERINE BUDIG
New Nork Times Bestselling Author of *Aim True* and Internationally Renowned Yoga Instructor

HITTING

ROCK

MIDDLE

SALLIE HOLDER

HITTING
ROCK
MIDDLE

THE ROADMAP FROM EMPTY SUCCESS
TO TRUE FULFILLMENT

Advantage.

Published by Advantage, Charleston, South Carolina.
Member of Advantage Media Group.

ADVANTAGE is a registered trademark, and the Advantage colophon is a trademark of Advantage Media Group, Inc.

Printed in the United States of America.

10 9 8 7 6 5 4 3 2 1

ISBN: 978-1-64225-119-7
LCCN: 2019917126

Book design by Megan Elger.

This publication is designed to provide accurate and authoritative information in regard to the subject matter covered. It is sold with the understanding that the publisher is not engaged in rendering legal, accounting, or other professional services. If legal advice or other expert assistance is required, the services of a competent professional person should be sought.

Advantage Media Group is proud to be a part of the Tree Neutral® program. Tree Neutral offsets the number of trees consumed in the production and printing of this book by taking proactive steps such as planting trees in direct proportion to the number of trees used to print books. To learn more about Tree Neutral, please visit **www.treeneutral.com**.

Advantage Media Group is a publisher of business, self-improvement, and professional development books and online learning. We help entrepreneurs, business leaders, and professionals share their Stories, Passion, and Knowledge to help others Learn & Grow. Do you have a manuscript or book idea that you would like us to consider for publishing? Please visit **advantagefamily.com** or call **1.866.775.1696**.

To Paul, Edward, and Catherine:
This book is for you, my heart and soul, and the ones
I'd fight to break out of Rock Middle for every single day.

ACKNOWLEDGMENTS

To me, nothing can be created entirely alone. We all need support along the way to make our dreams come true, and this book, my dream, would not have been possible without the tremendous amount of support I've received from so many.

I'll never forget sitting in my office just a few years ago and sharing this crazy dream with a woman I hardly knew. There was something about Heather White that made me dream bigger from the start. From that point forward my life was headed in a new direction—a bolder trajectory. Heather turned out to be just the believer, encourager, and coach I needed in my life. She saw who I was capable of becoming before I did and has since ridden with me along the many waves of highs and lows of making it a reality. I cannot thank her enough for her wisdom and her generously kind nature. I hope she'll celebrate the significant role she played in helping to make this possible.

I've had another mentor along this journey too: Wendy. She's been a rock for me both personally and professionally. She's seen me at my worst and encouraged me to be my best. She too has believed in me and taught me so much. In fact, I share some of her lessons in the book, as they had a dramatic effect on my perspective on business.

Nobody has been more important to me in the pursuit of this project than the members of my family. My twin sister, Stacy Smallwood, has also been a business mentor to me along the way.

She's gained a tremendous amount of perspective on entrepreneurship during her fourteen years as a business owner. She so generously shares that perspective with me whenever I need it, no matter where she is in the world. She gave me the daily encouragement and words of wisdom I needed during this writing process! She has spent countless hours sharing her energy (both emotional and physical) with me. She's my rock, and I'm better at what I do because of her. I love you, sis! Thank you from the bottom of my heart.

I also want to thank my parents, whose love and guidance are with me in whatever I pursue. They've seen me make some pretty bold choices over the last several years, and yet they were always there for me asking, "How can we help?" The thing was, they'd already helped. They instilled in me a work ethic and discipline that I got directly from them, and it's been such a gift to rely on throughout this journey. Most importantly, I want to thank my loving and supportive husband, Paul, and my two wonderful children, Edward and Catherine, who provide unending inspiration. I do everything for the three of you. You make my life feel complete, and I love you all with all of my heart.

CONTENTS

THE NIGHT I HIT ROCK MIDDLE

> Can you remember who you were before the
> world told you who you should be?
>
> —DANIELLE LAPORTE

It was the greatest night of my life. As I stood at the podium at the city's conference center in front of a thousand people, accepting the Young Professional of the Year award from the chamber of commerce, I was certain of that. I was twenty-seven years old. I had already been named one of the "Best and Brightest 35 and Under," and this was just another feather in my cap that I felt I still needed. As I listened to the congratulatory applause, I took pride in my latest accomplishment. Everything I had worked for—from straight-A report cards since grade school to graduating with honors from Vanderbilt University to earning my law degree—had culminated in this moment. I was officially successful.

Mere hours later, I lay curled up on the bathroom floor sobbing, unable to sleep, wondering how I had managed to screw up my life so royally. I didn't know what to call the realization I'd had following the ceremony, but now I have the words for it: I had hit Rock Middle.

No one could say I had hit rock bottom. No way. I was what I had set out to be, a successful attorney with a major law firm. I was earning a great salary and was well respected by peers and clients alike. But this evening, I had been hit with the awareness, like a thunderbolt, that it was a hollow victory. I was bereft because the awards and money meant little compared to the sudden, shocking realization that a long time ago, I had set foot on a path without thinking about who I was and where I wanted to be at the end of my life. That path had led to great success, to this evening, and to the swift but sure knowledge that I was stuck in the wrong place. I was in Rock Middle. I wasn't failing, not at all, but I wasn't where I was supposed to be, doing what I was meant to do—that's what I knew in my gut for sure that night. And that realization was devastating.

Since you're reading this book, you may be feeling stuck in Rock Middle, too. You might be in the middle of a long, successful career that feels a little less than spectacular. You might be someone who has changed jobs frequently, always hoping "this one" will be the right fit, the one that brings you more satisfaction in your career. Or you might just be starting out, anxious that you haven't made the right choice, that you too will end up stuck one day. You are likely to be a woman, for a million reasons we'll discuss later, but men also find themselves in this place.

I'm happy to say I can help. I hope to save you a lot of time in getting to where you are meant to be—even if you aren't at all sure where that is right now. I didn't get there overnight, nor will you. But it won't take you ten years, as it did me, to become who you were always meant to be.

I am not here to say that you need to accept or adapt. Quite the opposite. I am here to coach you on changing your life, if that's what you desire. Change isn't easy. Change creates growth, and there will be growing pains. But those growing pains are positive. The pain of standing still is not.

We'll examine how the imprinting of our parents, our teachers, and our social norms during childhood has shaped our beliefs, habits, and patterns. Looking at the things that influenced your decisions from childhood on will help you cut through the clutter and be both more realistic and more optimistic about your future. These things have potentially created a feeling of disconnect, because when you're following an external model that differs from who you are internally, this prevents you from being your authentic self. This disconnect might have made you choose another path without intention, and before you knew it, you were on a ten-year detour away from your real purpose, just as I was. We'll also look at how easy it can be to get stuck. The fear of aiming too high and making the wrong decision or of discovering we weren't actually capable of being bigger are the chains that hold us back.

> CHANGE CREATES GROWTH, AND THERE WILL BE GROWING PAINS. BUT THOSE GROWING PAINS ARE POSITIVE. THE PAIN OF STANDING STILL IS NOT.

Don't fear change. You're not going to start chapter 1 as an advertising agency vice president and close the book ready to take your punk band on the road in a trailer. Not every change needs to be extreme. Some of the subtlest changes can make the biggest difference. On the other hand, I hope some people tap into their dream and decide they want to take the plunge and change drastically. Whether you feel stuck in a career you love or hate, you can find out if what you're investing your time and energy in is right for you: the internal you that's authentic, not the external you other people see or say you *should* be.

Most important of all, this is a chance to put down your armor, if you've been using it to protect yourself as I did, and dream again, completely free of judgment. It's a chance to dream without others thinking you're crazy and, hopefully, without you judging yourself or your worth. What I've learned is how quick we are to judge ourselves and then believe the negative things; later we'll discover exactly why that is too. Discovering and defining your dream without these negative beliefs is an inspiring and transformational activity that will be one of the first steps on your new path. It's a chance to dream the way you did as a child, boundlessly, knowing I'm here to support you in making it a reality. So if you did want to be the punk rock band singer, we can figure it out together. I'll walk you through the steps to consider and how to get started.

You might be thinking I've lost my mind to encourage such changes, and maybe you believe it's totally unrealistic. If this sounds scary, don't panic. It's a voyage of self-knowledge. I'm not trying to change you into something you don't want to be. I want you to be set free from the invisible influences that might be holding you back. Give yourself the gift of openness and willingness. Be open to new ideas and willing to try them. As Albert Einstein said, "We can't solve our problems by using the same kind of thinking we used when we created them."

This doesn't mean that anything any one of us has done in the past was a waste of time. It took me ten years from that award night to strike out on my own, but during that time, I was gradually unsticking myself and heading toward my dream. I'm grateful for what I took away from the past: a dedication to hard work and valuable skills. When I look back on all of it, I know that was the path I needed to take to get where I am today. I don't want anyone to feel regretful. Whatever you have done in your life has brought you here and given you the determination to become the best version of yourself. I believe you got here because this experience of getting unstuck needed to be part of your journey.

It does mean that along the way you gathered details about yourself you believed to be the solemn truth, and during this process, we will challenge those thoughts. These beliefs can make our load lighter, lifting and energizing us, or they can be a weight that keeps us held where we are. Seeing our decisions and desires objectively is the key to building on the good and banishing the bad. Once we can do that, we can proceed in a new direction with increased confidence as we create the type of plan and commitment everyone needs in order to get started.

If you're now thinking, *That sounds great, but it's not for me; I want professional growth, not personal,* don't jump off the train so fast. I get you, because I've been there. Trust me, this process is for you. I've learned that the only way to achieve the professional success you seek is to understand how you got to where you are and grasp the patterns and habits you follow that may be holding you back. Once you have decided which habits have propelled you and which have held you back, you can begin the professional growth you desire.

> ONCE YOU HAVE DECIDED WHICH HABITS HAVE PROPELLED YOU AND WHICH HAVE HELD YOU BACK, YOU CAN BEGIN THE PROFESSIONAL GROWTH YOU DESIRE.

Maybe right now you feel sadness or dissatisfaction for what seems to be no reason. You're in the right place for that, too. Those feelings result from not being who you were meant to be. Over time, as you force yourself to stay on that external path, the disconnect between who you are on the inside and who you show the world you are on the outside grows, as does your sadness and dissatisfaction.

If you're thinking, *But nothing has held me back. I have a great career, and I'm successful at what I do,* then I would ask you to consider the question, "How could it get even better than this?" Part of the reason I hit Rock Middle was because I lacked the belief it could get any better. I want everyone to believe it can always be better and that they deserve to go after it.

Finally, if you have experienced (in your own way) the same pain I did that night when the excitement over my award win collapsed and sent me crashing into my "fetal position on the bathroom floor" moment. I can say this to you with confidence: you're going to be fine. I suspect that, rather than deconstructing the causes and trying to find answers, you may have been dealing with any feelings of dissatisfaction as I had: by either stonewalling or not openly admitting your fears. Maybe you've tried to resolve your situation by using the same thought patterns you used in creating that situation. And here you are. Albert was right.

All it takes is a bit of courage and the willingness to get started. You've already done that. I'm not saying it will be a piece of cake. Getting in touch with your dream and the habits and thinking that have kept you from making it come true can lead to some painful moments. Some scary ones, too, as you confront your own fears and challenge yourself. That's why I'm here: to guide you through the process. And at the end of it, you will have a plan for your new life.

I'm going to show you how to:

- Dream again by following facts versus feelings.

- Approach setbacks with curiosity to envision your new future.

- Step out of the either/or paradigm.

- Let go of excuses that are merely obstacles to success.

- Accept that the next step is the only one you need to take to run with it.

These are the five essential tools to help you stop staying stuck in Rock Middle and start doing what you were meant to do!

My dream—when I finally discovered it—was to be able to help others, especially women, get there faster than I did. It's why I decided to write this book. This book is my way of giving back, of helping others quickly master what took me so long to formulate and achieve. It's for you, but it's meaningless until you fill in the blanks and do the work. I hope my personal story, which I'll share as we take this journey together, will help you. I'll also be sharing the stories of clients, people who went from mumbling, "I don't think I can do it. This just isn't for me," to exclaiming, "I did it, and I've never been happier!"

Yes, it's work, but it won't be in vain, and it won't leave you feeling let down, disappointed in yourself, or deciding that you are helpless. You will be inspired and take away valuable lessons from the stories of others, real people who overcame their trepidation and the habits of a lifetime to get themselves out of Rock Middle. They did it, and I know you can. Here is what it will be like when you find the dream within you and embrace it.

BEFORE	AFTER
I often feel disappointed in myself and depressed by the life I created.	I'm content and enthusiastic about my life.
I feel little joy in going to work and less satisfied with my accomplishments.	I am eager to get started every day and excited about the future.
I take pride in being so successful, but everything seems routine and dreary.	I'm busy and active, with a full life. I love taking on new projects.
I'm eager to be liked and often reluctant to speak my mind.	I feel confident, knowing the value I provide to others through my expertise and not afraid to speak my truth.

Best of all, you don't need to give anything up but an outlook and (potentially) a job that haven't been fulfilling. You just need to make some investments of time and, depending on your dream, perhaps make some financial and lifestyle adjustments to get started. But your return on investment will be enormous, personally as well as professionally.

When we're done here, you might decide that you've found your niche already but want to give it a needed twist you hadn't previously considered to advance in your career. Maybe you decide you want to split your time and energy between two different careers, both of which will fulfill you in their own way; maybe you decide that you want to make the long-buried dream you discovered during this process the reality of your life. Whatever you decide, my goal is for you to take away new skills and insights that will make anything you do more satisfying and rewarding because you'll know it's what you were meant to be doing all along.

CHAPTER ONE

LET'S GET HONEST WITH OURSELVES

> Real transformation requires real honesty. If you
> want to move forward, get real with yourself.
>
> —BRYANT McGILL

I used to be you.

I knew something was wrong, but I couldn't even name it, much less know what to do about it. I was trapped in my own career, by my own choice, and I didn't know how to escape, only that something had to change.

It took me ten years after the night I accepted my award and had my bathroom floor moment to get out of the trap I'd created for myself. You don't have to wait that long to create the life you want. In fact, let me help you save time, trouble, and pain. It's my goal to help you find a better way. It's the way that doesn't bring the hollowness of achieve-

> THIS JOURNEY WE'RE
> BEGINNING ISN'T TO THE
> CENTER OF THE EARTH;
> IT'S TO THE CENTER
> OF YOU.

ment. The answer isn't out there in the ether. It's been inside you all this time. This journey we're beginning isn't to the center of the earth; it's to the center of you.

Where are you now?

What's your current reality? Here's a hint: it's likely not what you generally tell people when they ask how you're doing. "Things are fine. All great here. You?" Nope, I don't want to hear a superficial answer. I get it. On the outside, I was saying, "I'm happy, of course. My career's going great. What more could I want?" That's what I thought I should show people, while inside I said to myself, *I may hate what I'm doing, but I should be grateful for what I have. How dare I try to find something more satisfying? How dare I consider doing something else?* I felt exasperated and disheartened because I realized a huge disconnect existed between what I showed the world externally and who I was internally.

That's how we convince ourselves to settle for the middle. I had unconsciously convinced myself it would be selfish if I tried to make a change. I'm here to tell you that settling for the middle—even if it's a comfy middle with high income, awards, and prestige—isn't worth it. For me, trying to do that made me feel less worthy, less confident, and as if I would never accomplish enough to feel successful. Even worse, I felt trapped. That all finally changed for me when I took a long and honest look at myself.

It's the dig-deep, move-you-to-tears, honest look at yourself that will make a difference. For example, when I was at Rock Middle, my honest look at myself would have sounded like this:

> I'm unhappy, like deeply unhappy. I feel it in my core. I cry sometimes when I'm alone. I can tell it impacts my day-to-day life. It makes me feel like I'm crazy sometimes. I share it with no one because I'm not sure what to say, and frankly,

I'm afraid I'd start crying if I tried to explain it. I just know there's a happier, thriving, cup-overflowing version of me out there, and I have no clue how to become her.

If we were sitting on the couch together talking about where you are now, what would you say? It's hard to go there, I know. But it's important not to skip this step. We've got to get really honest with ourselves. When we don't, I find we're willing to accept less than our greatest potential. We tend to be willing to compromise and allow certain parts of our current reality to hang around simply because they aren't completely miserable. Right? They're tolerable. Well, that's *not* what we're going for now! We're not going for a life that includes a different version of Rock Middle. We want to create something extraordinary!

In order to do that, we have to be 100 percent honest about what's not a "Hell, yes!" in our lives. The goal is rooting out anything that doesn't make you say, "Hell, yes, I want that in my life and can't wait to do that." They're our lives, but somewhere along the way, we forgot we were in charge of making the choices. As you get honest, make a list of everything that's a "Hell, yes!" in your life. Anything that doesn't go in that column becomes a "Hell, no!" We'll be speaking more about those.

When Did You Last Ask Yourself Why?

Now, how do you create the future you once imagined? The one you still subconsciously wonder whether it still exists within you or if it's even still possible at this point? The answer to that is emphatically yes, it still exists, and it's completely possible. Let's do it together.

First, you need to ask yourself, "Why?" As in, "Why did I get here?" When I ask coaching clients that question during our first meeting, they often start with an explanation of their dissatisfaction with their current career or most recent job. They're sometimes surprised when I tell them to go back further. You see, your work history is only part of the puzzle. Like me, you have certainly made many career decisions based on habits, fears, and beliefs cultivated from childhood on. Whether consciously or not, when we're young, we put ourselves inside boxes of what we can and cannot do. We use those boxes to make decisions about what types of careers we go into. We stay safe inside those boxes without being fulfilled, not even being aware of **The Box**. Sometimes we aren't even aware of our own distress until something happens that causes a crack in **The Box** and lets the reality of our lives in. We suddenly see our current reality, and we don't like what we see. Whenever I saw my current reality, that's when I wanted to cry the most. I felt sad and disappointed in myself.

Even though we feel unhappy with our current work, it's rarely the core issue. It's a symptom of being stuck, not a cause. What causes us to feel stuck are the habits, beliefs, and fears that dictate our actions and create our current reality. Let me give you an example. If you engage in the habit of repeating to yourself the belief that you are not good at sales, you won't seek out opportunities to engage in sales or improve that ability. You'll create the fear that if you have to do sales as part of a particular job, you'll fail. Therefore, you hold yourself back from applying for positions you'd otherwise love, simply because there's a sales component. Do you see how this one decision you made about yourself, likely based on no concrete facts, dictated your actions and thus your achievements?

The best thing we can do now is look at where those decisions came from by reaching back and answering questions about our life. The answers will help you discover why you made the decision to choose this path.

Do you know the habits, beliefs, and fears that keep you stuck? If so, great—write them down. But if you don't, let's answer some critical questions to discover yours. Try keeping a journal throughout reading this book. Just grab any notebook, write down these questions, and think long and hard about the answers. Be honest. No one else needs to see what you put down.

In answering the questions below, think about why you made each choice. Do you remember? Did you choose to be here intentionally, or make decisions based on some belief that it would lead you somewhere great? Or was there a fear that if you chose another path, it would lead to something detrimental?

- What did you enjoy doing as a child?

- Have you continued that passion, or did you stop? If so, why?

- What did you want to do/be when you grew up?

- Why did you want to be that?

- Why did you choose the college you went to?

- Why did you choose your first career?

- What have you always said you're incapable of doing?

- Why haven't you pursued your dream thus far?

- What do you believe will happen if you leave your current career?

- What do you believe your current career says about you?

- Did you ever start to believe you weren't capable of doing something and never cease to believe that?

- Since then, have many of your decisions been based on that limiting belief?

And then simply keep asking, "Why?"

It's the why behind the answers to those questions that tells you the most. The answers often reveal if and when you made the decision to believe in your limitations more than your possibilities.

As you write down your answers, think about and look for limiting beliefs, habits, and fears that have continued throughout your life. This is what I call the "stinking thinking" that has gotten and kept you stuck. These limiting beliefs are the thoughts that constrain us and tell us we cannot do something.

The good news is your abilities are not fixed. You can learn and get unstuck from the habits, beliefs, and fears that are controlling your growth and future. It simply starts by stopping yourself from repeating the stinking thinking and replacing it with the truth: that you're capable of anything you believe.

My Stinking Thinking

I used to be a very different person. I didn't let myself believe anything was possible. I had a lot of bad habits and an abundance of limiting beliefs, and I spent a lot of time feeding my fears. As I look back over the course of my life, I can see exactly where my stinking thinking began.

My father has his MBA; he was, and remains, a very successful real estate developer. Throughout my life, he was consistently in positions of leadership, whether it was as the chairman of the board of trustees of a large bank, public university, or our private school. My mother was the first woman to manage a bank in the entire state of South Carolina. She was a stay-at-home mom when I was growing up, but she remained a high achiever.

The expectation at our house was that you were going to be

the best and excel at everything you did. We weren't forced to do anything, but I felt that failure wasn't an option. My parents never said those exact words, but my assumption that it was an expectation colored everything. I was programmed for success. I religiously followed my parents' suggestions for my life, from what sports to be active in to where to apply to college to attending law school. There was a right way to do things and a wrong way. So the idea that I had control over my own life was a foreign concept to me. I never gave credence to my wishes; often I didn't have any because I was so dependent on external opinions.

What reduced me to my bathroom floor moment almost a decade later wasn't a lack of external approval of my career or my awards. What struck me that night was that I had done all of this for them and not for me. By "them," I mean other people. I had done it to gain their approval and acknowledgment, to reach their idea of success, and that was impossible. No one could give me enough approval or recognition for me to *feel* successful.

See, after the big award ceremony, everyone moved on to something else. My success wasn't the big deal I had expected it to be. People acknowledged it and moved on. The problem wasn't them. It was inside of me. It was my focus on the approval of others rather than on my own happiness that had gotten me here, to the realization that all the awards and success in my law career couldn't make me genuinely happy. I hadn't done any of this for me; I just did what I thought I should be doing, following a habit that brought me no real joy. It began in childhood, and I had unknowingly kept feeding it all the way to Rock Middle.

I went to law school because since childhood, I believed—from movies, television, and society in general—that guaranteed success and prestige for a woman were achievable through only a few careers, and a lawyer or a doctor were definitely on the list. My choice was law. I chose to become an attorney, and I never looked back, not for years. So when I finally did, it was devastating.

How do we buy into our own lies about what success is? How do we become the accomplices to our own unhappiness? We'll examine this because a clear view of our complicity in our dilemma is a necessity for change. But what I realized that night through my tears and misery was that I had fallen for, and enhanced, an insidious lie of what success was supposed to look like. And I couldn't see a way out.

I told myself I had no other skills. I believed 100 percent that all I could do was be a lawyer. When I tried to think about change, the options were narrow and unappealing: I could own a law firm or become a general counsel inside a large corporation. I didn't see my hard-earned skills as *translatable*. The lie I told myself was that I was good at doing one thing and that if I did something else, I'd be giving up on success. That belief dictated my actions and therefore my unwillingness to change for way too long.

Getting Stuck Is Common—Here's Why

You're not the only one who gets stuck. So many women get stuck. I did, and I imagine you're reading this book because you did too. We tend to get stuck in what I call **The Loop**.

The Loop is a process you experience each time you try to conquer your stinking thinking. Each time you start a new adventure, you hope the experience will be different than the last. But because your beliefs sneak back in after you get started, they convince you not to change, not to take steps to be happier.

In order to change, you need to break **The Loop**.

The Loop begins when you start feeling excited, when you start thinking, *Maybe this is it! I could do something different, and this is the thing that will make me happy.* But your stinking thinking has been in place for so long you begin to look for evidence that doing something different could lead to disaster, and you tell yourself you're researching just to make sure the change isn't a bad idea.

The evidence convinces you that whatever the change was, it's not right for you. You get discouraged and stop looking for possibilities. You put that idea away and suddenly believe you were crazy for even considering it! You say things like, "That was a dumb idea anyway. I should just stay where I am and learn to love it." You stop and stay there until all of a sudden, by some miracle, another idea strikes, you get inspired again, and the process starts all over.

The Loop

What we never realized is that when nothing changes, *nothing* changes. We never stood a chance of breaking out of **The Loop** and believing in our dream while following the same methods we'd used in the past. We were always operating under the same old habits, patterns, and beliefs. Now you can identify it for what it is—falling back into stinking thinking.

We were searching for evidence that our ideas or dream wouldn't work, and we will always find evidence of whatever we're looking for in our lives. It's no wonder we always made our way back to staying the same. We've got to break up with stinking thinking if we really want to create change in our lives.

I remember when I was stuck in **The Loop**. I always felt an emptiness, something missing from what I was doing, but I consoled myself by simply working harder and believing the next accomplishment would make me feel better. I thought the "something missing" was more achievement. Like you, I wanted to make real changes but didn't know how or even why. My lack of self-confidence convinced me it was all in my mind and that I should just stop and count my blessings.

Still, intrigued by the feeling that I could do more with my life, I would go to a talk or seminar and get fired up, thinking, *I could do this! This might be perfect for me.* Then I would research and research until I got discouraged. Unconsciously, I was looking for what I would finally find—information that told me, "See, Sallie, you can't do it! It's been done already." I thought I was seeking affirmation, but all the time, I was just seeking to confirm my doubts. I was in danger of being a Looper for life.

I'm here to help you snap out of that. I want you to think outside of that self-defeating loop. **The Loop** leads us to search for a reason to quit, a way out. Why? Because the fear is overwhelming. We are so frightened of the unknown, of not knowing how it's all going to turn out, and the unknown feeds the fear. We want assurances before we get started. But that's not how it works. There are no promises that can be made to make us feel secure enough to take a chance. So we stay stuck in **The Loop**.

The Brain Is Part of the Problem

Don't worry, you're not entirely to blame. Your brain helps you stay stuck too. I've found it critical to understand that we're wired to stay stuck. It helped me free myself to create change when I knew it wasn't entirely my fault. Here's how the brain is part of the problem too.

Imagine yourself at the edge of a wheat field, with tall stalks in front of you as far as the eye can see. You look to the left and see a well-worn path that has already been created, so walking in that direction looks easy. The stalks lie flat on the ground, and you can get started in that direction right away. You look to the right and see nothing but stalks—no path exists in that direction. Your brain looks at that well-worn path and tells you, "Go down that well-worn path. It's easy," and you immediately think, *That path has to be the best one for me.*

We make the assumption, based on our feelings, that if the path exists, it must be the right one. Your brain tells you that creating a new path will be dangerous and too difficult—that you'll be vulnerable, you'll go broke, people will view you as a loser—whatever it takes to convince you not to go outside the same path you've been down a million times.

But creating that new path in the wheat field, the one no one else has gone down, is inherently none of those things, not yet. It isn't dangerous or a career-destroyer or the road to poverty or the lion's den. It is merely a new path. It's your opportunity to discover what's right for you without interference from anyone else, and to explore what other options exist for you that you may never have considered before now.

Think about your career. How many other careers, ones that might be a better fit for you, have you really explored? How many opportunities have you looked into to gauge what the actual potential income could be? How many have you explored fitting into your life part time, so you could give it a shot, save up, and make the transition gradually?

If your answer was "none," you are not alone. We defeat ourselves because we live and base our decisions on feelings, not facts. We assume we already know the facts—that the new career will be too hard to start, too risky, won't produce enough income. But those aren't factually true—they're just feelings. They're feelings based on a trip down the old, well-worn path that our brain convinces us to take because the new path would create danger for us. You're starting to get the gist.

> WE DEFEAT OURSELVES BECAUSE WE LIVE AND BASE OUR DECISIONS ON FEELINGS, NOT FACTS.

It's a biological fact that our brains are programmable. When we have told ourselves, or others have assured us of, the same thing over and over again, it sticks. That's how people end up being in sales or technology or teaching and don't know why: somewhere along the way, someone said, "That would be good for you," and the longer any of us follows that path, the more firmly our brain tells us, "You can't afford to change. You've reached a certain level doing what you do. Why would you want to start over? Think of your marriage! Think of your children!" And as women, we tend to stop thinking about ourselves. We don't feel we're worthy, and suddenly we're stuck. Our brain wants to shield us from pain and protect us, but it has just been keeping us stuck because we didn't know better. Now we do!

Now is the time to challenge those habits and beliefs. Let's throw everything you think about yourself on the table. Imagine the phrases "I can't sell/speak/change careers/earn more," or whatever it is you say that limits you, are now on the table, and together we're rewriting what you're capable of doing. We're only pulling out those phrases that serve you and are accurate. It's time to eliminate those assumptions you've made about yourself and start over by believing you can do anything.

Use Your Why to Guide You

I know it isn't easy to let emotions go. We tend to let our feelings overwhelm the facts. The fact is, you can make a change whenever you choose. You just have to know your why! Contrary to popular opinion (more of the well-worn path), you don't immediately need to know how—just why.

Trying to get started on your own without your why is like searching for things in the dark. You fumble around with only a vague sense of what's in front of you because you feel lost. You quickly shift your focus to *how* you're going to get to this new place, believing that knowing *how* will allow you to see the path. But if you can step back and think about why you want to make a change, you won't be fumbling in the dark anymore. Who do you want to have become by the end of your life? Who is it that you want to be remembered for being? What do you see yourself being/doing when you're finishing your career? The epitaph on your grave won't list your accomplishments. It will say who you became during your life.

Hopefully you can see clearly the life you have now and understand why you want to change. Knowing why turns on the lights so you can find your way. Then it serves as a compass for where you're headed in the future. As Simon Sinek said in his book *Start with Why*, "It's those that start with 'why' that have the ability to inspire those around them or find others who inspire them." You'll stay inspired and keep your business moving forward if you keep your why at the forefront of your mind.

My why is to help people who aren't happy in their lives or careers have the courage to ditch society's version of success and create their own. It's why I do what I do and why I believe I'm on this earth. I found a way to alleviate the suffering I felt and create the happiness and success I always wanted. Now I get to share that journey of getting to the truth of who you were meant to be with others. My why is leading me closer to my ultimate purpose and helps me determine the work I do that supports it. Write down your why now, so that you can use it as your guide for the future.

You might already, deep down, know your why. Maybe it's been clouded by what other people think you should do or who you should be. Maybe it's buried under all the fear whispering that you can't or shouldn't budge. But it's there, and once you bring it out into the light, everything gets so much easier.

Think of your why as your map into the unknown: a map of the wheat field, perhaps, one that will lead to a better path than the well-worn one. A map, after all, is the thing you can come back to when you need help getting where you're going. You wouldn't decide to drive cross country and then just jump into the car and head off. If you did, we can agree it would take you a lot longer to get where you wanted to go. Using your why is like taking the map with you as you drive. It eliminates the detours and wrong turns and gives you the clearest path to your ultimate destination. It can be scary to follow your why, but it will always be the shortest path to where you want to go.

Don't get me wrong. It's not always smooth sailing just because you now have a map. You can still try to talk yourself out of trying to reach your ultimate destination. *It's so far to go*, you might think. *I'll just stay here. It's not so bad.* But you don't need to drive nonstop.

Looking too far ahead and trying to project how it will all go can be self-defeating too. If you were on that long trip, you wouldn't know when there would be traffic or how the weather would be because so many of those things are unpredictable. Yet we spend a ton of time today trying to predict the future and how every leg of our journey to our why will be, look, and feel. Spending all our time today obsessing about the future is called "future tripping." You wouldn't want to waste a minute of your trip, so don't waste a minute of your career on it either. You need to keep in mind that you're heading to your dream one step at a time. You can't get there any faster, so keep your eye on your destination and allow yourself to be more patient about the process of getting there.

Once you know your why, you can evaluate if you're doing things simply because they're on your to-do list or because they're leading you to your ultimate purpose. If the work isn't leading you closer to your purpose, then you'll know the plans you had were made out of habit or someone else's definition of success. Eliminate the to-do list items that lead you down that same worn-out path, and create new ones that will take you closer to your why.

Breaking Free of Either/Or

I know change is possible because I went through it myself, and one of the key mental shifts is eliminating the either/or paradigm we have in our heads.

I had a client who was much like us. She was programmed to

believe success looked a certain way externally. She was in residential real estate. She was doing very well but worried she didn't have the right processes in place for her business's continuing growth. She sought my help to establish the processes she believed she needed to reach the next level of success. We went through the typical questions, those I just asked you, about what and why. I heard her mention the word "should" several times, which clued me in that something was off. "I should this, I should that" are sure signs someone is not making decisions based on their own internal needs but following what they believe are the external rules of society—what we *should* be doing.

I could tell from the beginning there was another aspect to her, something else she wasn't telling me that made her happy. My spirits soared when she texted me to say, "You know, I actually like to perform comedy too." Clearly this was what was missing. She had always believed a choice had to be made between a career in comedy and a career in real estate, and the responsible choice was to pursue a real estate career. She had the habit of looking at the situation as either/or: either she'd be in real estate, or she'd be a comedian. That habit prevented her from being able to achieve her ultimate purpose. Do you see now how our habits and beliefs keep us stuck?

Together, we worked on the development of both of her careers because together they light her soul on fire. We came up with a plan of how she could enrich her life by pursuing every aspect of herself. After all, why not? Why is one career expected to fulfill every aspect of who we are, anyhow? She loved real estate, but she also loved being a comedian. She had simply become stuck looking at her future through a single-minded, dutiful lens.

She's now a comedian/real estate agent. Today she's happier and more confident, and therefore she's far less attached to the outcome of a real estate sale. When you're doing what you love to do, you don't care what anyone else thinks. You know it's right. The result of making this choice? She's selling more, earning more, and working less. There is great freedom in knowing you're doing what's right for you. Happiness and confidence are what every woman gets when she fulfills her internal desire, and when she isn't searching for external approval anymore.

> WHEN YOU'RE DOING WHAT YOU LOVE TO DO, YOU DON'T CARE WHAT ANYONE ELSE THINKS. YOU KNOW IT'S RIGHT.

A big part of being able to let go of that external approval is understanding you don't have to choose. You don't have to live with one or the other. You can create a "both/and" situation, just as my client did. If you can eliminate this either/or thinking in your life and career, you can have the freedom to create any dream your heart desires, even one including comedy and real estate.

Your Freedom Starts Now

What does this mean to you as you begin this journey? It means that defining and following your dream doesn't have to mean choosing between stability and sacrifice. That's how it's often presented, especially in the movies: it's a huge sacrifice in order to follow your dream, always involving a "risk everything" leap into entrepreneurship. I jokingly say, "You'd better not be leaping. I don't want you to leap anywhere!" Why? Because leaping means skipping over important steps you need to learn in the beginning and the middle in order to end up where you want to be.

You don't *need* to leap into making some massive change, so don't push yourself. You just need to begin the process of exploring change, getting honest, and letting go of the stinking thinking that has been holding you back. Often when people immediately focus on the end, on such a dramatic picture of change, they defeat themselves. They start thinking, "Omigod, that's so different from where I am now that I can't possibly know if it's right for me." (Yeah, welcome back to **The Loop**. Come on in. Take a seat. Stay awhile.)

Others might make the leap and land on their feet, but because they've skipped all the vital learning steps, those all-important early and middle parts, they fail. Failing sets off the fear alarms and encourages them to retreat back to—you got it!—their safe and unfulfilling place in **The Loop**. They could have taken one step and another while making a gradual transition, but noooooo, they were in a big hurry to get where they wanted to be at the end. Their haste brought them right back to where they had been all along—only more reluctant than ever to change.

This isn't a problem just for those in corporate careers, either. Creatives struggle too. So many people have told them along the way that their dream is never going to amount to much, so they won't give themselves permission to follow it. They keep hearing, "You'll never make any money" or "You know how few artists/writers/singers/dancers/take your pick make it?" and "You can do that when you're done with your real career!" I also hear, "It would be selfish of me to pursue my dream because I'd be robbing my family of the income generated by a real career."

I say, "What if the opposite is true? What if the selfish choice is failing to pursue your dream?" You were put on this earth with a God-given talent that only you have and can give the world. Aren't we robbing the world of your talent if you don't pursue your dream? Aren't we robbing the world of the talents of other creatives when we discourage them from following their dreams and pursuing their talents? In my humble opinion and personal experience, one reason our depression rates are through the roof is because so many people believe the lie, stay stuck, and never break out of **The Loop** to see their dreams are possible.

We've put everybody in a box and told them, "Be the same. Here's what you can do for a career. Here's what you can make money doing," but that's just based on repeating more of the same. It's simply more of what everyone else has already done.

We want them not only to be the same as everyone else, but also the same at forty as they were at twenty! It's funny, because everyone loves so-called overnight success stories shown by the media, while few people in the real world encourage people to follow their dreams. We just like it when we watch it on TV because it reminds us for a minute that dreams can come true. The stories are inspiring: choir singer Susan Boyle finding fame and fortune even though she came in second on *Britain's Got Talent*; Adam Lambert becoming a big star on *American Idol* and now as a member of Queen; Whoopi Goldberg being a desairologist, applying makeup to bodies in a funeral home; Lucy Liu having a career as an aerobics instructor; Hugh Jackman teaching physical education.

But we don't hang on to and use the lessons from their stories to take action for ourselves. We don't grasp that they succeeded because, at some point, they realized what they were meant to be—and because they *tried*, put aside all of their stinking thinking, broke free of **The Loop**, and took the risk of putting themselves out there. That's the lesson here. They found their dream, and you can too.

What I've discovered is that the people who have given themselves permission to follow their dream are like unicorns—I'm not entirely sure they exist, but I like to believe they do anyway. We are all given signs throughout our careers and lives that say to us, "This is what you were meant to do." The unicorns heard that message, listened to it, and lived it. Now it's your turn. So go for it! It's never too late.

Start by finding the habits and thought patterns that have come back again and again in your life, the times you stopped yourself from going for your dreams, or the first time you said something was impossible. Didn't go out for the cheerleading squad? Applied not to your first choice of colleges but to your second, third, and fourth? Never asked for a raise or promotion because "they'll give me one when they're ready"? Considering looking for a new job, but at the same level in the same type of company, doing exactly what you're doing now? Look for decisions that have put you and kept you in **The Loop**. Stop conditioning yourself to believe that the well-worn path is the only one that leads to happiness, while any other will leave you stranded in the woods with the bears. Ask yourself how you have personally grown and changed since you made your decision about what you wanted to be back when you were twelve or twenty-two.

In the words of the Dalai Lama, Tenzin Gyatso, "The purpose of our lives is to be happy." I did it, and you can do it, too.

YOUR ROCK MIDDLE REMINDER:

You are worthy of following your dream. It may be the most selfless thing you could do.

CHAPTER TWO

UNLEASHING THE DREAM WITHIN YOU!

The future belongs to those who believe
in the beauty of their dreams.

—ELEANOR ROOSEVELT

H ave you defined your dream? Don't worry if you haven't. It's there. Everyone has a dream. It may have slipped away from you while you were doing what you thought you should, but that doesn't mean it isn't still locked inside your heart and mind. Together, we can find it and set it free.

I want to make this clear: when we talk about your dream, I'm not talking about "following your dream" in a clichéd, motivational manner. I'm not a motivational speaker or writer here to give you a pep talk. I'm someone who wants to provide practical business advice to make sure you're giving your top talent to whatever you will be doing in the future. That being said, I'm also here to tell you that dreams really do come true if you recognize, define, plan, and work toward them.

I'm here because I'm tired of seeing people doing something

completely against their dreams merely because external voices told them it's the path they should follow.

As you now know, I did that, and it got me to two places: first, a hollow feeling of success, and second, crying on my bathroom floor. But as I traveled to the first place, got my law degree, practiced law, and gathered my awards, on the few times I stopped to ask myself, "Do I even like this?" I answered with, "Oh, that doesn't matter."

I'm here to tell you, it does matter.

What you do with your life and whether or not you're spending year after year in your career doing what you were meant to do matters a great deal. It affects you every day; it impacts your family and your own happiness. Defining your dream and choosing the path to making it your reality is choosing happiness. It's that simple. I've always loved how Shawn Achor, the happiness researcher, defined happiness in his book *Big Potential* by saying, "Happiness is the joy you feel striving toward your potential."

You see, when you get to do the work you're meant to do, simply being able to do that work will be fulfilling to you. You will no longer be sacrificing your happiness to pursue some external goal. You will lose your attachment to the outcome because your internal feeling of contentment won't rise and fall based on whether or not a client says yes or no. You will be happier, and as a result, the things you wish for will gravitate toward you more and more. You will achieve them—without losing your authentic happiness. They will be more fulfilling than ever when it's done this way, when they come to you as a result of you following your real purpose.

For a long time, I let the rewards convince me that I was living my dream. Once those no longer fulfilled me and I was sitting in my unhappiness, I realized I had justified treating myself because I believed my sacrifice deserved a reward. It's easy when you're successful and miserable to build a high life on whatever soothes you temporarily, be it shopping, luxury vacations, alcohol, or drugs. All of them can be dependable accomplices in helping you justify not changing. I created my own vicious circle, telling myself I was staying because I couldn't earn as much doing anything else, then spending all that extra money rewarding myself for doing what I didn't want to do. Amazing how something so convoluted can be so easy to slide into. That's the comedy of it. I was rewarding myself for my sacrifice, but the rewards didn't cut it. The words "retail therapy" are always said tongue-in-cheek, because everyone knows the therapy isn't real. All the designer clothes in the world couldn't cover the self-inflicted wounds; no five-star restaurant could alleviate the true hunger and fill the hole in my soul. It was insatiable. I felt like that next thing— the external—would alleviate my lack of happiness internally. But I was always wrong.

Eliminate the Expertise Trap

Maybe you have never given in to the big-spender trap, but **The Expertise Trap** is one that few of us are safe from. I say that as someone who was held firmly and miserably back by it until I finally had the courage to fully be myself.

The Expertise Trap is that insidious feeling of being too good at what you're doing now to change. You're too savvy an attorney, too skilled an accountant, too damned great at getting one failed company after another back on its feet as CEO, too seasoned at whatever it is that bores you to tears to *do anything else*. We tell ourselves that we are going to get up enough nerve to change, and then we decide on a lateral move instead: a new law or accounting firm, an expansion of our medical practice to a second location, another version of the same role in a different sector. That's not true change but leaning in to your expertise, believing that the setting was the source of those feelings.

We not only fall into **The Expertise Trap**. We are its creators. My gosh, I can't tell you how many times I would tell myself I needed to break away and do something different, but I never spoke about it. I presented myself externally, to anyone who could have helped me, as the person I still wanted them to think I was. It was as if I were silently begging, "Please, tell me what else I can use this law degree for," all the while announcing, "This is who I am. This is the only expertise I have. This is what I want to do for the rest of my life."

I may not have been open with friends and family about my feelings, but I was willing to tell every kind of coach and therapist that existed. If there was someone out there I could pay money to in the hope that they'd tell me what to do, I saw them. I wanted to have someone else tell me what I could be doing—someone externally informing me again. Remember, I still believed all the answers came from someone other than me. They always had.

I took the Strong Interest Inventory test from Myers-Briggs. I was pinning my hopes on its helping me. I figured it had to; after all, their report describes your personal style preferences and ranks your most compatible occupations from a list of 260 jobs. *Aha!* I thought. *Now I'm going to find out what I should be doing.* After all, Myers-Briggs has built a very successful business letting people know what they're best suited to do.

My report came back, and as I looked at the top of the page, all I could see were the words "Classic Entrepreneur."

My response? "Are you serious? This is useless. I don't want to open my own law firm, and that's the only expertise I have." That was the end of it for me. Experiment over. **The Loop** rejoined. I simply could not get out of my own way. I could only see the limited beliefs I had about what I was capable of doing with my life.

If I had done the exercise we went through in the first chapter and listened to my responses, I would have known what I should be doing. When I was seven years old, my mom set me up out on the street with some of her old furniture to sell because I was so excited to make my own money. I went on to make a lemonade stand and work it every summer, long after it was "cute" for me to be out there, because I loved the entrepreneurial feeling so much. Next, the lemonade stand became a homemade jewelry stand. You get the gist. I had been a classic entrepreneur since first grade, yet I denied, denied, denied. My belief in **The Expertise Trap** was so strong that I couldn't see any career besides being a lawyer.

Some people spend an entire lifetime not realizing their dream. We know that, right? We've all heard stories of people sadly saying, "If only … " And whatever they add to that phrase, the meaning is invariably, "If only I had gotten out of **The Loop**," or "If only I had been conscious enough to break out of my habits, beliefs, and fears." I often remind myself that no one ends their life wishing they had taken fewer chances. Their end-of-life wishes are always that they'd done more of what they loved. Remembering this keeps me going in times when I don't want to break out of **The Loop** or take a chance. Thinking through this helps remind me that regret comes from not taking the chance. You don't have to be one of those people. No one has to be. Getting in touch with and letting go as you pursue your dream is the key. We waste much more time and energy resisting our dream to stay in **The Loop** than we do building a career based on our dream.

Your Gut May Be Right

We often feel that indescribable feeling within that encourages us to take a chance. In fact, as you look back upon how you got to here, you will undoubtedly recall a time when you were tempted to stray from that well-worn path and risk starting out in a new direction.

I call that feeling **The Tug** (I know, original, right?).

The Tug is when something internally makes you think, "I could do that." Have you ever had that feeling? I'm sure you have. You've likely ignored it or dismissed the feeling in the past as illogical, but I would argue **The Tug** is the key to finding what you're meant to do or where you're meant to be. If you get quiet and listen to yourself and your desires, you'll likely be able to find your dream by identifying what you feel **The Tug** internally to do. It's that inexplicable feeling you should pursue a particular career or project that's often well outside your comfort zone. If you've struggled to identify your dream, start here. Drown out the voices and opinions of others, and listen to your own guidance. It will never lead you astray.

The real estate agent who wanted to be a comic had **The Tug**. She felt an internal desire to pursue comedy, but she had always been too frightened to do anything about it. Even when she broached the subject with me, she did it in a text rather than saying it out loud.

Once she went where **The Tug** led her, she was working from a place of abundance and fulfillment. She no longer felt the feeling of scarcity that comes when you're not following your dream, and she prospered. In fact, by dividing her time between real estate and comedy, she closed more real estate deals in the first quarter of 2019 than she had in all of 2018! If you're doing what your heart and soul desire, every part of your life will benefit.

Remember, she came to me seeking help to grow her real estate business, ignoring **The Tug** that told her to do stand-up comedy. She was standing at the precipice, ready to run full tilt in real estate, thinking she needed more tools in order to take on more projects. But the panic of needing more income from her real estate business wasn't based in reality. It was based on believing she needed more externally to fulfill her internal emptiness. The world always tells us that it's more money we're missing, and if only we have more money, we'll be happy. Once we discussed whether that was actually what she needed and what was missing, she realized more money wasn't what she was really after—it was a feeling of fulfillment she craved. She realized what was actually missing was that permission slip to pursue her other passion, comedy. When she combined her passions, she flourished more than ever.

I'm not a believer in having to sacrifice income if you choose to follow your dream. I hear it all the time—people saying they would love to follow their dream, but they can't afford it or would have to make significant changes in their life, like selling their home. Attaching such negative consequences to following your dream would discourage anyone from taking action. Is it actually a fact, though, that you will have to experience such detrimental things if you choose to follow your dream? Or is it more likely a feeling created by the stinking thinking intended to discourage you? Creating a dream career and having a great income are not mutually exclusive concepts. You don't have to choose one or the other. In fact, I believe, and have found it to be true consistently, that your income will grow in proportion to your happiness. When happiness leads and is made the priority, then success and income will follow.

The real estate agent/comedian made happiness her priority. She took the risk, devised a plan, and incrementally began to build her career in comedy. She continued to sell property but without expanding the business, at least not while she was letting **The Tug** take her where it might. If her real estate business suffered, she could always back off from her comedy pursuits. However, as I had expected, she was soon making more money in real estate than she had previously, all while pursuing her dream of comedy. Her happiness, like a magnet, had drawn more of the same to her. We fear taking the first step toward our dream because we create such extreme consequences, but the facts are that the scale doesn't swing so far in the other direction. You can want more and have it without negative consequences. Her **Tug** led her in the right direction, and I'm confident yours will too.

You Deserve More Than a Participation Trophy

Some of the fear around following **The Tug** exists because it might mean you're breaking away from your current mold. Declaring a bigger dream can be scary. It triggers self-centered fear of not getting what you want or losing something you already have. Oftentimes we believe what we'll lose is our ability to fit in with everyone else, and we settle for fitting in instead of standing out.

When I was pondering the question of why people are so afraid to ask for more in their lives or take action to pursue something bigger, I couldn't help but wonder if, in a world where everyone gets a trophy in T-ball, where average is often rewarded as good enough, and where everything is supposedly wonderful (at least on the outside), we've inadvertently said there's no need to dream bigger.

In our world of social media, we share a lot about how our lives resemble everyone else's and worry about leaving anyone without an award. In our Instagram and Facebook images, we see everyone's representation of a perfect life. The problem there is that it creates the desire for conformity and a fear around standing out as different or less than perfect. We live in an environment where it's easy to feel like breaking out of that mold would be criticized. There's no way you're going to say you want more or are unsatisfied with what you have, because you already have so much, you have what others perceive as good, and declaring you want more might make other people feel bad. Plus, good is supposed to be good enough. You have no reason to complain or be dissatisfied with your life!

The opposite of that, the antithesis of staying in the middle, would be having the audacity to dream bigger and to have your own way, your own vision of success that doesn't look like anyone else's. Being the person that actually gets first place (and earns a danged trophy).

The reality is that everyone can't fit into one mold. And why would we want them to anyway? That's not the way we were made. The idea of conformity, of living our lives in **The Box** of what success is supposed to look like, will slowly kill us. Eventually I think it leads us to feeling as if we want to burst, dying to break out of the strait-jacket we're living in and scream.

The stifling effects of our participation trophy culture aren't limited to people scrolling social media, either. They've also crept into the teamwork aspects of business today. Sure, it's great to be on a team, but if no one is recognized for extra effort or superlative work, the end result is a dearth of accomplishment and creativity. When everyone wants to be seen and appreciated yet is unwilling to stand out from the rest, the result is stagnation and a lack of growth.

Women especially fall prey to the participation trophy culture by downplaying their accomplishments. When praised, our instinct is to say, "Oh, it wasn't just me. It was a team effort." Seriously? This is not the right answer. That would be, "Thank you." Full stop. No justification needs to follow. We should never feel guilty. After all, the others on the team made their decisions, too, and maybe they decided just so-so was good enough. We're so worried someone will hate us if we don't recognize or acknowledge everyone. You may as well own your accomplishments, because believing other people will like us if we choose to stay small is a misassumption. You can't control another person's opinion of you, no matter how small you become. Who's to say staying small will guarantee their approval, anyway? Yet we base huge life decisions on this and trust that being liked will take us where we want to go instead of trusting our own internal desires to take us there.

If you're feeling **The Tug** toward something more, it's absolutely okay to say, "Good enough is not good enough for me!" Do it now before you want to scream. Take that first step. It's totally okay to not know what that next thing is yet. Most of us spend so much of our lives living the lie and trying to be satisfied with good enough; it's going to take a minute for you to allow yourself to get used to dreaming bigger!

And if you aren't instantly inspired, if you don't already know what that big dream is, it doesn't mean it's not there. They're two very different things: 1) having **The Tug** and the desire for more and 2) actually being able to identify what that desire for more translates into. My belief is that **The Tug** wouldn't be there if it wasn't meant for you. Just because you haven't experienced enough growth yet to identify what that **Tug** really means doesn't mean you're wrong to feel it. It just means you haven't found it yet!

So if you're feeling that **Tug** toward something more, consider this your permission slip to start exploring becoming that bigger, bolder version of yourself. Once you find what it translates into, you'll be able to walk away from any kind of participation trophy and head straight for the win!

Rediscovering Your Dream

What if you don't know where to head at all, though? What if you try and try but can't nail down your dream and want to shrug it off, to say, "I guess I just didn't have a dream," and stay in the safety of your comfort zone? That won't fly with me. I'm *that* sure the thread still exists, and the dream is still there. It may be buried, but it's very much alive.

You need to do three things that might sound averse to one another, but trust me, they aren't. First, you need to relax. Take a walk, meditate, get in a receptive zone. Next, think about the why questions again. And finally, brainstorm. Blue-sky it radically. Let your mind go, and write down anything that comes into your mind as a career you could love. I don't care how ridiculous it sounds to you. Astronaut, brain surgeon, restauranteur, sailor, architect, tinker, tailor, spy? Let your mind run free, because it's sure to run into something out there that jogs your memory about something you once loved or who you once wanted to be.

I have a client who rediscovered his dream through this process. He had always loved art, but somewhere along the way, he'd made the assumptions that men couldn't be artists and that men simply didn't do art for a living.

But as we talked about his past and I asked "Why?" to dig deeper into the choices he had made, facts started replacing feelings. He told me he'd chosen a college based on their advertising program. He admitted he had been interested in another college, one that valued art, but in the end, he chose not to attend it. Again, I asked, "Why?" His answer was the key: he said there had been a family friend who exemplified success when he was growing up. This man had all the trappings that came along with success, and he was in advertising.

Thus the choice was made and his dream forgotten.

And there you have it. All these decisions sprang from the belief that men couldn't be artists, combined with fear that art wouldn't lead to the same type of success afforded by a career like advertising. By the time he sought me out, he had been running a successful printing company for some time and had increased its success, but he wasn't happy. It was his fallback, and deep down inside he knew he was at Rock Middle.

He continued to do what most at Rock Middle do, driving out the thoughts and feelings that they're not fulfilled. They make themselves busier. They take on duties, expand their role, sure, but all the time they're accepting immobility, not advancement. He was thinking, *Well, I'm just not going to love what I do. I need to accept that and move on. I need to work as hard as I can.*

This is how we sabotage our dreams. It's as if you're saying, "If I just put my head down and accept the misery, it will just go by faster." Is that what you want? I'm sure it isn't, because you're here with me on this journey. Maybe you've been trying to talk yourself into a lateral move. Maybe you've been planning your retirement far in the future because you don't picture allowing yourself to do something you enjoy before then. You need to know that you were never meant to stop at Rock Middle. It was supposed to be no more than a pit stop on the way to the pinnacle of your career. Keep asking yourself questions to explore what's at the root of your dream. If no one else's feelings could be hurt, who would you allow yourself to become? That question often leads to a little rediscovery. I hope it does for you too.

You Have the Time to Find Your Dream

This client was so busy filling his time, he fell into the common misconception that he didn't have the time to rediscover his dream. How could he, with all his obligations and his other career? The time does exist, but it needs to be used in a new way. If you're making yourself feel better by being busy, busy, busy all the time, too busy do this or that, so busy it hurts, you are leaking energy that you could be using to build your dream! All these thoughts and "settling fors" are is a colossal energy leak.

The fact is your energy is being split right now. One part is being applied to keep yourself busy and ignore your dream, and another part is being spent on the thoughts that tell you that you cannot do it. If you redirect the energy you're throwing at those things back to your exploration of your dream, you'll gain back a lot of time (and energy). When people start to realize how much time they're throwing away every single day through these energy leaks, and how much time they could gain back by stopping that behavior, they grow in courage. We all become more courageous when we stop fooling ourselves into believing, or pretending to believe, that we're happy doing what we don't want to do.

By the time you finish this book, I hope you will be able to articulate your dream. I hope you will be able to see how you can utilize that gained time toward building the future you desire. In the case of the artist, it took just a few more questions to put him firmly on a new path, because they challenged him to see his truth. "Do you think it's 100 percent true that men can't be artists?" I asked. "And if it's not 100 percent true, then what could you be?"

"I could be what I always wanted to be." *Bingo.*

Not until these realizations surfaced was he able to see that he'd never been interested in advertising at all—not until at last having reached Rock Middle and deciding to take action. I'm pleased to say he immediately started working on the transition to becoming the artist he had dreamed of being. Even better: his sales tools will prove invaluable in helping him market his work. He's happier at the printing company, too, knowing that he won't be there forever, that he's on the way to doing what he had always longed to do. He's standing on the shoulders of the previous success he's had. He's not abandoning the skills or knowledge he acquired along the way. We all have threads running throughout our careers, threads of past endeavors that will help us realize our dream. Now he's using his threads to his benefit.

Believing we have to keep on doing what we have been doing is a false assumption. But so is thinking that our past career was a colossal waste of our time on earth. Trust me, that's a feeling, not a fact. Each of us has a career thread running through our lives, and it has nothing to do with whether we were in the perfect place or not. It's simply about the translatable skills we picked up along the way and other lessons

> WE ALL HAVE THREADS RUNNING THROUGHOUT OUR CAREERS, THREADS OF PAST ENDEAVORS THAT WILL HELP US REALIZE OUR DREAM.

we have learned. For instance, I brought to my second law firm my knowledge of labor and employment law. That knowledge helped me succeed there, as it had at my first job, but it also laid the groundwork for the business coaching I do now. The COO positions taught me a lot about running businesses, even though I never envisioned how that knowledge would come in handy in a completely different way in the future. My early speaking engagements showed me that I was in my element talking to and helping others, that I had a gift for simplifying complex ideas and making them easily digestible. My success in sales and sales training brought me a whole different set of skills: I learned how to analyze and give guidance on common problems and to inspire women to grow and become successful.

As I was acquiring these skills, I was skeptical there was a thread pulling them together. They seemed so different, and it seemed illogical that they would all lead to the same destination, but they did, and they will for you too! You might not see the thread while you're acquiring the skills, just as I didn't. You may have to see it in hindsight, but what you can do now is put trust in the process—the process of life. Trust that you're being led in the directions of your dream when you follow your intuition and when you don't hold yourself back from making the difficult choices because of things like fear.

Every time I meet someone who, like me, chose to be someone they were never meant to be, I see their dream still within them. So even if, like this man who once yearned to be an artist, you haven't felt **The Tug** toward something for years, even if you never considered what it might have been until you felt stuck and looked to this book for help, you can still find your dream. It's strong enough that it has survived.

If you have been ignoring your own **Tug**, if you have been hugging it to you like a shameful secret, you can start freeing yourself the moment you say it out loud—even if it comes out while you're making plans to stay in Rock Middle. Admitting the dream to yourself is the first step, and I know it isn't easy.

I understand, because I am so aware of the years before I had defined my dream or even worked up the courage to attempt to do so. All those awards I had won? They didn't comfort me or make it less scary for me to say, "I want to be bigger."

"Any path you choose will likely be long and full of ups and downs, so choose the one that brings you the most joy and makes you feel most alive." Hilary Swank said that, and she could have been speaking to you. Remember, you pass this way only once, but that doesn't mean you're ever too old or that it's too late to let your dream decide your future.

YOUR ROCK MIDDLE REMINDER:

Even if you haven't found it yet,
your dream is waiting for you.

CHAPTER THREE

YOU'VE GOT THE POWER!

Embrace the glorious mess that you are.

—ELIZABETH GILBERT

When did we get so scared of change? Why did we start acting as if we needed anyone's permission but our own? Somewhere along the way, we started to feel unworthy of our dream. We allowed our stinking thinking to convince us it was never going to happen. I say this from experience, from having let that fear get the better of me for nearly a decade.

I decided to practice law because I thought success meant having a title that other people respected. I was an attorney, a law school graduate. That made me proud, as did those awards I worked so hard to earn. I fervently chased those external markers of success, and I was good at it. I externalized everything, as if I were playing the role of "Sallie Holder, Attorney-at-Law." I was good at that too. Few people, if any, ever suspected that my career was not what I really wanted or that it had never felt the way I thought it should.

There was a catch, of course, to playing that role. There were always consequences that went beyond a lack of emotional fulfillment. I started to feel the physical side effects too. That version of success looked like exhaustion at the end of each day. It looked like not wanting to get up every morning. It looked like putting on makeup, pulling on pantyhose, and giving up open-toed shoes, which were "unprofessional," because I was girding myself with the armor of female success. That version of success? It looked like being somebody other than myself. And it felt like pain. Have you ever felt that pain too? The pain of all those compromises?

I spent years telling myself that these were necessary compromises, minor in the grand scheme of things. Maybe you have too. I convinced myself they were necessities I must accept in order to reach and maintain success. Sound familiar? What they all really were was a big fat lie fed to me by my feeling of unworthiness, a lie of what success was supposed to look like according to society's rules. I believed that lie, which gave birth to more lies. Once we have those doubts, it can feel so hard to change, to get started, to define our dream. Of course, we can't, because we're trapped by measuring our success with society's ruler rather than our own.

Since I was waiting on others to define my success, I was also waiting on their permission to make a change. It was as though I wanted someone to come and pluck me out of obscurity, like they do on reality TV shows, and say, "This is where you belong." But what I know now is I didn't need that to change. I could do it on my own, and you can too. Yes, it's hard to make a change, because it requires courage, but you can't just wait for someone to come along and give you a permission slip: Permission Granted to Be Your Authentic Self. You don't need anyone's permission but your own. So if you're looking for someone to say it's okay to find and follow your dream, consider this permission granted!

The Foundation to Get Started

Giving yourself permission to grow means letting go of other people's ideas of success and keeping your own approval foremost in your mind. Once I knew the law wasn't for me, I lost a lot of my identity. I had to redefine what success would mean to me, and I had to believe I was worthy of it. In my years since following my own dream—coaching women to achieve theirs—the biggest roadblock I've seen, time and again, is the feeling of unworthiness. So many intelligent, creative, and motivated women can't get started because they don't actually feel worthy of their own big dream.

The unworthiness doesn't show up as you might think. Rarely do people say, "I'm unworthy." That would be too simple. It shows up as phrases like "Who am I to think I could do that?" or "I could never" or "That's just a silly dream." Sounding closer now to something you've said? What I've realized is we should be saying, "Why not me?" Your shift in belief here is critical.

Your belief in your big dream is the foundation for your future success. You want that foundation to be sturdy, wide, and unshakable despite whatever comes along. It should be like the bottom layer of a pyramid. It holds up the rest of you. This belief in yourself means you believe you're capable of creating anything you desire. It shows that you know you're too great, too smart, too hardworking to settle for anything less than an extraordinary life. This level of deep belief in yourself comes from creating the habit of repeating these statements to yourself more often than those associated with stinking thinking. This belief is a muscle you'll need to exercise. It may be weak right now, but you can build it through effort. Once it's strong, you'll have it to support you through anything you face in life and in business.

If I had believed in myself in the way I suggest you should, I would have realized there wasn't something wrong with me and made the change long before I did. Instead, as is not uncommon, I looked for an immediate solution. I couldn't give myself permission to create drastic change, so I made a lateral move, believing it would be the fix to my feelings of unworthiness. Lateral moves come from looking at short-term gains that rarely provide the long-term solutions we crave. They feel like middle ground between where we are and the big moves we don't believe we deserve or are capable of achieving. But they rarely are the answer.

The first lateral move was to get more involved in speaking and training opportunities within my law practice. I started traveling a lot and taking as many speaking engagements on employment law as I could, because that was the area in which I felt most like myself. I remember thinking, *If only this were a career! I could do something like this.* Can you believe it? It didn't even occur to me to give myself permission to try to create a career like that. It didn't fit into **The Box** of the few things I saw as successful.

So while I was miserable being successful for the third-largest labor and employment law firm in the country, I came up with lateral move number two as a possible solution: working for a small law firm. I took a position serving as their chief operating officer. I was still practicing law, but it gave me the chance to be in a more family-friendly and forgiving environment in a five-person firm instead of a seven-hundred-person one. Oh, sure, it was me being in a large firm that was the problem, not the work I did day in and out. I know, it seems hilarious that I didn't see it.

This is what we do when we feel trapped, without realizing we're simply switching cages. I had wanted out of the position I was in so badly, and my brain wasn't giving me solutions, so I sought advice from other people. They would say, "Well, you can be a general counsel. You can be an attorney for hire. You can start your own firm. You can go to a midlevel firm." Yes, The Trap of Expertise was at work no matter where I turned. Are you seeing it now? Every single thing I was offered or that anyone concerned with career counseling suggested was always in the area of expertise I had previously gained. Never once did anyone say to me, "Your skills are translatable to anything in the world you want to do. What makes your heart happy? Where do you want to end up at the end of your life?"

I think if someone had questioned me, had asked, "What comes naturally to you? What have you always loved?" I might have discovered that public speaking, training, and coaching was that thing. I couldn't blame anyone else. It wasn't as though I was honest about how genuinely unhappy I was, and I was still so stuck on my lack of belief and limited expertise that I couldn't fathom anything else. So many of us get trapped in this expertise bubble of being certain that what we started with at age twenty-two ought to be what we're still doing at forty-two. That's how I stayed in **The Box** for so long, and why so many other women are still in theirs. We see our expertise as valuable, but solely as it applies to our current profession. We don't believe that we are genuinely capable of anything else.

Women are especially self-sabotaging when it comes to change, which is no surprise, since so many of us grew up receiving choice-limiting social messages about what our career options were. I refer to these as The Lie of the Seven Careers (yes, I have a nickname for everything). There are others, but when I was a teenager, these were the main careers that I remember girls being encouraged to choose from:

- Doctor

- Lawyer

- Teacher

- Nurse

- Librarian

- Secretary

- Homemaker

These were our options. I chose one and stuck with it because that's what we did. Young women have more choices today, but a lot of them continue to shoot too low, scared to identify with a big vision because they're worried about failure and what it might take to get to where they want to be.

Men aren't worried about *almost* achieving their vision. They don't waste time asking if they're worthy of their dream. They look at every step completed, including getting most of the way there, as success, while women perceive not getting all the way to our ultimate goal as failure. We succeed at the careers that don't excite us because we're too frightened to give ourselves permission to try succeeding at those that do. That has to stop. We can make the choice now to believe in our dreams and start going after them.

> WE SUCCEED AT THE CAREERS THAT DON'T EXCITE US BECAUSE WE'RE TOO FRIGHTENED TO GIVE OURSELVES PERMISSION TO TRY SUCCEEDING AT THOSE THAT DO. THAT HAS TO STOP.

If you don't deal with the lack of belief, you'll continue to make moves that keep you inside your own **Box**. That's what I did. I found myself bored all over again at the small law firm, because the move I'd made wasn't outside **The Box**. I would look out my office window and think how much I wanted to be out there and how little I wanted to be sitting in the same place years from now. Luckily a college friend came to town and said, "You should be part of this sales company I work with." I wasn't even about to consider it. Me? Sales?

"I'm a lawyer," I said. "I need something else in law." I couldn't picture anything beyond the walls of **The Box**. I wasn't happy, yet I was comfortable in my job because it was well inside my comfort zone. I was scared of being uncomfortable. I didn't yet realize that growth *should* feel uncomfortable.

"The sales company is having a get-together tonight," she said, ignoring my dismissal. "You should just come by and see what it's like." She told me the name of the restaurant where it was being held—just as I was driving by it. Kismet? That coincidence pulled me into the parking lot, thinking, *Why not?* I had nothing to lose by checking it out.

That's how I made my first nonlateral move. For the first time, I opened myself to the possibility of something outside of practicing law. After learning more about the woman-owned, woman-centered company and realizing I could work as an independent contractor while continuing to be COO, I took the job. The work attracted me because it was finally a new challenge, letting me sell and help others develop their skills.

I did this for three years while staying on with the law firm. I coached women on sales tactics, showed them how to become entrepreneurs. I traveled the world and lived a life that was filled with rewards and recognition. I loved every minute of it. Until I didn't. It hit me like a ton of bricks. I was still in **The Box**. *Oh my God*, I thought, *how the hell have I done this again?* My feeling of unworthiness had led me right back to the same place. I needed help.

By my fourth year of working at the sales company, I had left the

COO position behind to be a full-time entrepreneur. The experience was different from what I had expected. I felt lonely and uncertain. I loved the recognition, but that was more of the external and didn't fulfill the internal. See, throughout my time at the sales company, I hadn't increased my belief in myself. I had simply continued the search for external recognition. Let me assure you once and for all that you cannot become who you were meant to be—the biggest, boldest version of yourself—without doing the work to believe in yourself.

> LET ME ASSURE YOU ONCE AND FOR ALL THAT YOU CANNOT BECOME WHO YOU WERE MEANT TO BE—THE BIGGEST, BOLDEST VERSION OF YOURSELF—WITHOUT DOING THE WORK TO BELIEVE IN YOURSELF.

I felt I had to make the best of this because I'd made the drastic change. It had to work. I couldn't possibly make another change. Mostly, I was scared, afraid that I would never do anything I loved, never find my role. I didn't know how to grow this belief in myself on my own, even though I'd tried. I couldn't find a guide on how to become the person I was meant to be, and left to my own devices, I knew I would make the same old mistakes. When someone suggested hiring a business coach might help me see things in myself I couldn't see, I was all ears.

Getting Help in Your Growth

Not everyone needs a coach. You can accomplish a great deal on your own by following the guidance in this book without any more financial investment. But coaches can help too. If you're concerned with how you're going to fare through this stage of transforming your beliefs, a coach might be right for you too.

Coaches act as catalysts to force you to stay outside your comfort zone. They encourage you to step out of your current reality to see new possibilities. Almost every successful CEO I have listened to or read lately has indicated that a professional business coach has been instrumental in the growth of their business and their decision-making processes. They don't ask their best friends or family for advice. People you know would be affected in one way or another by your making a change, which tends to make it hard for them to encourage it. A coach doesn't have their own vested interest in the outcome of your decisions. They can more easily encourage change, as it won't directly have an impact on their lives.

The importance of not just stepping out of your comfort zone but *staying* out there cannot be overstated. A coach creates space for you to grow, even when you doubt it can happen. A good coach sticks with you to hold your hand and help you stay in the path of the unknown. You need to go all the way through the transformation process, and it's easier with the right person by your side. The only way to the other side is to get through it, and a good coach will light your way.

One of the truest statements my coach ever made was, "There are people out there doing exactly what it is that you want to do right now, with less expertise and less talent than you have, and they're making millions of dollars doing it. That's simply a fact." It was the space she created and the change in my belief that gave me the courage to find my true why. Working with my business coach changed the possibilities I saw ahead of me. It challenged my notion of unworthiness and convinced me those seven careers weren't my only options. Most importantly, I learned to have patience with the process and realized I could give myself permission to dream as big as I did as a child.

We all have to come to our transformation in our own time. We can't rush the process. Developing this belief in yourself is much like the transformational process of a caterpillar turning into a butterfly. If you were to pull the caterpillar out of its cocoon early, it would never be able to fly. Its wings would be unusable. Allow yourself the time to develop every aspect of yourself before you get started with the drastic change you want to make, and you'll fly when the time comes.

Once you have that belief in yourself, the gift of curiosity will help you figure out where to go next. Jen Rubio, of Away luggage, used curiosity to find her way. Without a university degree, she worked her way to one covetable position after another with major companies. She traveled constantly, working for leading international brands as a marketing expert. Then one day her suitcase broke. She was curious as to how she might fix the problem of shoddy luggage, something about which she knew nothing.

In the meantime, she was offered a VP of marketing position in New York for a top brand, her so-called dream job—or so she thought—that she'd always been working toward. But her newly considered luggage idea had created a fresh **Tug**; she wanted to see where it might lead her. Still in her twenties, she had the gumption to turn down what was a guaranteed journey to external success because she was curious and daring. Creating her own company had not been a longtime dream, but when **The Tug** told her where to go, she gave herself permission to do that. That's how she came up with Away, now a $100 million travel-and-lifestyle brand. She had her beliefs, habits, and fears in order, so she was ready to soar. She wasn't resistant to **The Tug**—and look what she was able to create.

This is what we can do when we believe in ourselves, follow our curiosity, and fly. Saying yes to our gut might not always work out, but most of the time when we ignore that **Tug** and say yes to the other thing, that thing turns out not to have been our dream anyhow. My dream for you, and all of us, is that we won't let our lack of beliefs or feeling of unworthiness stop us. Saying yes to yourself is saying yes to the future and ultimately to a more fulfilling life. We can all say yes to a bigger, bolder future.

You Are Allowed to Slow Down

For most of my life, I believed success was simply a measure of who worked the hardest—that if a person took on more projects than anyone else and worked more hours, they would be given the "You're a Success" award. So the more I put my head down and worked, the better off I would be one day. I would wake up one day and be anointed with the award. I was working myself to death thinking I'd somehow reach a better destination. Boy, was I wrong.

Productivity is never the measure of success. It's not a contest in which the person who can check the most off of a to-do list wins the game. We confuse being busy with being productive. Busyness blinds us to our fear of growth and keeps us in **The Box**, too. We've all been friends or worked with someone who can't even say no to lunch without launching into an explanation of how terribly, terribly busy they are or how nothing ever gets done without them. Forcing yourself to take on more work won't necessarily lead you to your destination any faster.

In fact, being so busy you refuse to take a break might prevent you from ever getting to the success you seek. Taking a break to get an ice cream, or whatever it is that makes you feel like you're taking care of you, is critical to reaching internal success. What I've learned is that it's nearly impossible to have the type of internal success we want, the success that's the foundation for everything else, without self-care.

We rarely make the connection between success and self-care, but the connection is clear. We need time off to generate the inspiration, creativity, and energy we use to fuel our businesses and ourselves. When we force ourselves to keep our nose to the grindstone and keep going despite feelings of frustration and exhaustion, we're working in a space that's likely missing inspiration, creativity, and energy. Therefore, the work takes longer. We have to work harder and for more hours to do the same work because we're missing those elements. If we had taken a break to give ourselves the care we so desperately needed and our bodies and minds craved, we would have refueled ourselves and likely been able to do the same work in far less time.

Self-care isn't optional. It isn't what we do "when we have the time." We have to prioritize it to prevent us from losing the unique aspects of ourselves that we add to our work. Try adding self-care to your weekly calendar now. Yes, I said weekly calendar. Creating space for yourself will have a dramatic impact on both your work product and your effectiveness. Trust me.

Self-care includes performing the type of work that fills your soul. At a recent workshop I led, one of the attendees, an artist, told me that she felt trapped as a portrait painter. She wanted to create watercolors, but the portraits paid the bills. I convinced her that she was working harder producing portraits she didn't care about than she would if she focused more on simply doing what she loved.

By taking a portion of the energy she'd put into painting portraits and directing it instead to watercolor pieces, she would be doing something she loved, and she would grow that revenue stream at the same time. If she gave herself permission to do that, she'd have more energy and more time. She would be operating at a higher level. I asked, if she were doing something she loved, wouldn't she be doing it with more passion? She answered yes, as she did when I went on to ask if she thought she could take that higher level of passion with her to talk to people about why she chose to do watercolor work. If she did, then she would get to share her enthusiasm rather than be a technician painting something for cash.

If you produce a product when you're at your best, you create something that's a higher-level product. You get to charge more. If you are simply grinding out work to complete it and check a box, you care little about the work. Therefore, in the long run, you will work less and earn more when you concentrate your time producing whatever you're most passionate about creating. If you expend all your energy by running too hard, you'll be exhausted at the end of each day. It's easy to fall into the trap of the hustle, even when making the transformation to being the person you were meant to be. Look at it this way: you don't have to hustle anymore now that you're in touch with your dream. You don't need to keep running from task to task. Society and our inner critic tell us we have to push harder and work longer than everybody around us, but that's not true. Now you know better, so you can do better. We need to treat our dream with the respect it deserves and not try to force our way through it.

Being afraid that people won't like what you do if you make this change and no longer hustle for your worth can be a barrier to growth. What if you do show up naked and vulnerable

> WE NEED TO TREAT OUR DREAM WITH THE RESPECT IT DESERVES AND NOT TRY TO FORCE OUR WAY THROUGH IT.

and someone rejects you? Where do you go from there? The worst that could happen is you go back to what you were already doing.

Anna Quindlen said, "The life you have led doesn't need to be the only life you have." We convince ourselves it is, only because we're scared. But when we give ourselves permission, anything can be accomplished, not as a leap into the unknown, but as a planned, reasoned evolution. Only we can change ourselves. No genie can do it for us. Intentionally making the transition is the key.

Abandoning ship and running in the opposite direction as fast as possible can leave you stranded in the middle of the ocean. Instead, you can begin to slowly allow yourself to grow in the area you had previously blocked off. And if you're not sure what to do next, just relax. When we push ourselves too hard, we run out of energy.

If you look at energy as a pie, everything you do takes a slice out of it. Remember our energy is limited. I often describe the twenty-four hours we have every day as an energy pie. It's finite, so we have to be very intentional about how we portion out each slice. We don't want to unintentionally throw away slices to things like worry, regret, or fear—all of those can take a hefty slice from our twenty-four-hour energy pie if we let them. You don't want to waste your energy on those things, so let's choose to use our time and energy much more wisely.

As for knowing what to do, well, you're breaking new ground, so who said you're supposed to know it all? Like me, you might be a high achiever, but pushing through won't speed up anything. When you're on the road to success, it should flow, with no forcing involved. After all, you're swimming *with* your own personal tide now, not against it. In the words of Oprah Winfrey, "If you don't know what to do, do nothing. It will resolve itself, and the next action will appear."

So often, we're so busy looking for the end-all, be-all solution to our being stuck—the magic solution—that we don't get anywhere. We're hesitant to make a move until we know it's the last one. I'm here to remind you that making the next move could be the beginning and not the end of the journey.

Beware of putting too much pressure on that first step out of the gate. It's not either/or. It's not "change everything in your life right this minute or stay here in Rock Middle for the rest of your days." Maybe your next move will be a transition career, or maybe it's something you do in the interim that takes you closer to your one true dream.

Join me in granting yourself permission to take that step. Don't take it hesitantly, but do take it patiently. Don't overestimate what you can do in the immediate future and underestimate what can do over the course of the next ten years. And whatever you do, don't wait for anyone else to give you permission to be your best self. Just say, "Permission granted," and do it now!

YOUR ROCK MIDDLE REMINDER:

Find and follow your passion, but don't rush it. Keep calm as you continue moving ahead toward what makes you come alive.

CHAPTER FOUR

HARNESS WHAT YOU'VE GOT AND USE IT FOR YOUR BENEFIT!

She was powerful not because she wasn't scared but
because she went on so strongly, despite the fear.

—ATTICUS

After developing the strong foundation of belief, you will likely feel motivated to get yourself out of Rock Middle. That's great. It's where I want you to be. But now comes the harder part: staying motivated. So often going to hear a motivational speaker is invigorating, exciting, and promising. When the speaker is finished, you can feel the electricity in the room and hear the excitement in the attendees' voices. Everyone in the room is joined through the kinship of a single thought: *I'm going to do this!*

Some do. Some go all the way with whatever the program suggested. They commit themselves to change, and they do it. More frequently, people start out with the best of intentions, but then they get busy or preoccupied or lazy or tired. Gradually, they sink back to the state of frustration or disbelief they were in before they got started. Have you ever wondered what the difference was between those who stayed motivated and achieved their goals and those who gave up? Why are some able to leave the seminar and never look back, while others seem to be plagued by all the things that have held them back in the past—the fear, the excuses, the procrastination, the drive toward self-defeat?

Motivation, *ongoing* motivation, is something *you can give yourself.* To begin, you need to remind yourself that your fear is a good thing. It means you're challenging yourself to grow. Feeling the fear is normal. I'm not sure who sold us the story a long time ago that feeling fear should be an indication something's wrong. I finally learned feeling fearful is the exact opposite of wrong—it's the indication I'm finally on the right path. After all, facing our fears and challenging ourselves is how we get better at all the things we never thought we could do in the first place, whether we're a kid earning belts in karate or an adult learning to speak a new language. The best thing we can do when we're urging ourselves to change and grow is to recognize and feel the fear and then keep right on going, knowing we will get past it farther up the line.

I'm surprised how much we (myself included) expect that once we get over fear the first time, it's never supposed to come back—that once we've walked through making a huge change or tackling a major new area of growth, we won't be afraid anymore. We say to ourselves, "Okay, I did it!" and we expect that we won't have to feel afraid when we take on the next big thing.

But really, each stage of growth is going to come with fear again because it's new and it's different. And when we move into unfamiliar areas, we're inevitably going to have to face all those things again. All the bad habits that you thought you were past will come back up! All the "I'm not good enough" and "I don't know what I'm doing" and "Maybe I shouldn't be doing this" thoughts that are trying to keep us small! And it feels very scary.

When we're pushing ourselves to expand into new areas and grow into the best version of ourselves, the fear is always going to come back. But it doesn't have to get so loud that it stops us. We just have to remember that the fear means we're headed in the right direction. And that's a good thing!

We see kids do this all the time. They don't think they can play soccer, but then they take it up, get good at it—and then suddenly they're bored with it. Right? We're the same. We get used to the thing that once challenged us, and then before you know it, it doesn't challenge us anymore. Then we start looking around for excitement and challenge, and we go out and try to find our joy. And when you do that, all the old fears come back into play, which feels really confusing. It feels like, "What? Why am I feeling like this again? I thought I was past this!" But having knowledge and awareness of fear doesn't mean you get out of experiencing it.

The critical thing at this point is the ability to cultivate trust. To reflect back on all the things you've done that you never thought you could do and trust that you're going to be able to do this one too. Whatever it is. And that you're not crazy for feeling the fear. It's totally normal, and it means you're growing into who you're meant to be. So my conclusion is that the best we can do for ourselves is to feel the fear and do it anyway.

Facts versus Feelings

Feeling fear is also just that—it's nothing more than a feeling. It doesn't mean your thoughts about how impossible it will be to realize your dream are actually true—they're just feelings. We make the assumption that they're real because they feel so real. And remember that the biology of our brain also tells us they're real in an effort to protect us from the lions and tigers and bears, oh my!

Here's what I mean. My feelings told me that transitioning out of law would mean certain things: I was a failure; I couldn't hack it; I would never make as much income as I did practicing law; I would be unsuccessful. But these conclusions I had drawn about what leaving law meant about me were all just feelings. They weren't facts. How do I know that? I can ask myself one simple question. "Is this statement 100 percent true?" Is there no other possible alternative? Can I make this statement with certainty? If the statement isn't 100 percent true, then it cannot be a fact; it must be a feeling.

I could not say with certainty that I would be a failure if I left the practice of law. It was just the feeling of failure that was keeping me stuck and trapping me in **The Box**. The fact is, people can be successful in many careers other than the practice of law. I could agree that was a fact. Once you agree the statement is simply a feeling rather than a fact, you can ask yourself, "What could be true if this feeling isn't true?" This question took the lid off **The Box** for me.

What could be true? It could be true that I could succeed at so much more than I once believed. It could be true that the opportunities for my career are endless. It could be true that my feelings were the only thing standing in my way of seeing the world of possibilities ahead of me.

The realization that I could let go of these feelings that I had turned into certain facts was like pulling a giant weight off my chest. I could finally see opportunities again instead of just obstacles. I run through this exercise of examining facts versus feelings often now. In fact, I draw a chart like the one below. It's just a simple "T" diagram that I use each time I start to convince myself something I want to accomplish is impossible. It's a quick way of reframing my thoughts and opening my mind to the opportunities that truly exist. I spend a few minutes writing down every feeling I have about a situation, like those feelings I mentioned above. I write those in the "feelings" column. Then I run through those questions again—"Is it 100 percent true? And if it isn't, then what could be true?" I write what could be factually true if I were to let go of the feeling. The "facts" column then might have in it, "It could be true that I could earn more in another career" or "It could be true that I could find even greater success in another career."

FACTS	FEELINGS

Now's a great time to grab your journal and add to it by answering these questions below one by one. Take the time to really step back to analyze your own fears, label them, and determine if you've been leaning on feelings to keep you stuck.

1. What is holding you back?

2. What have you done that shows you you're good at what you do?

3. What feelings do you have that get in your way? What negative things do you tell yourself?

4. Is each of the feelings/negative things 100 percent true?

5. For any one of those you decide isn't 100 percent true, what could be factually true if that feeling weren't a fact? Write out those facts that will help you combat that feeling or thought in the future.

Envision Your Future

Once you've created your facts versus feelings chart, let's skip ahead and envision your life when you have become the best version of yourself. I run into you in the grocery store and say, "Congratulations, you've become the person you always wanted to be." What does that look like, and how do you feel? Describe who you are in detail in the present tense.

Where do you see yourself without those negative thoughts and limiting beliefs? The sky's the limit as you dream here. When you're out of **The Loop** and **The Box**, you're capable of being and doing anything. You can be that person and have that life. Don't stop yourself with "how"; just stick to "what" for now.

For example, if you were the real estate agent/comedian, you might write, "I am a stand-up comic. I love traveling all over the country appearing in clubs, meeting famous comics I've idolized for years, and hearing people laugh at my own observations and jokes. I still do a little real estate work on the side, because I enjoy it, but I take on only properties that excite me. I prefer to spend my spare time working out, watching old movies with my fiancé, or relaxing on my own with a book."

Way to go! You just accomplished a lot. You've broken down the gunk that gets in your way, and you know where you want to go. At this point, hopefully you're feeling motivated and your motivation will continue because you'll expect these feelings to arise again as you become that person—and you will be prepared to handle them.

If you haven't been able to answer all these questions, don't worry. You can take as long as you need. The questions will be here for you. Take some time to relax, to let your thoughts run free. Picture yourself doing things you'd like to do. You don't have to answer all the questions yet. We'll be coming back to this in chapter 6 when we talk about reaching your goals. In the meantime, keep the questions close at hand, so you can look back on them often and add as much as possible to your answers.

I understand that at this point you might believe everything would be easier if you had a crystal ball to know where you're headed (I've wished for the same on occasion—okay, on a lot of occasions) or to better understand why you had to experience certain defeats or setbacks along the way. The thing is, when we take away the mystery of the unknown, we also take away the magic of the unexpected. So trust someone on the other side of things, who struggled just as you might be struggling now, when I assure you that it will all come together.

Everything you've ever wanted is being held in divine trust for you—at least that's what my amazing coach, Heather White, told me, and I found it to be true. The best news is, you can't mess it up.

It won't go away. It will always be there for you when you're ready to receive all that you're capable of being. Relax, trust the process, and know your skills will come together to aid in the creation of your dream.

In fact, every example in this book focuses on a person who realized their dream after perceived setbacks or "wasting their time in other careers": the comic who discovered her comedic skills in the upbeat touch she brought to real estate sales, the artist who is using his marketing and business skills in selling his art, the watercolorist who honed her attention to detail in painting portraits. No time or skill is wasted. Each has both practical and emotional elements. Think of the skills you've acquired during the journey, so you will recognize how they can help you in reaching the new goals you're formulating.

You're Not Supposed to Know How

Now that you've envisioned your dream and what your life could look like if you truly were to go for it, it's time to think about the goals you'll need to achieve that dream. It's easy to say, "Write down your goals," but it isn't always an easy thing to do, especially for women. We, as women, don't want to put a goal down on paper if we don't think we can accomplish it. I can't tell you how many times I've seen women freeze when asked to write down their goals, because they immediately jump past writing down the goal and start thinking about how they're going to make it happen.

We begin imagining the process of accomplishing the goal, and if we aren't sure how it will come together, we tend to avoid writing it down. But not knowing how is a good thing when you're goal setting. It's a huge misunderstanding of the whole goal-setting process to assume you must know how to reach each and every goal before you get started. Why in the world should you know how to do something you've never done before? You're forging an entirely new path. You say you don't know how because you don't have past experiences to rely on. But everything you've kept doing from memory is stuff you've *already* done. Now you're moving on to something entirely unfamiliar.

What all this means is that if a goal you're setting for yourself looks familiar, it isn't a big enough goal. Instead of saying, "I don't know how," say, "I can't wait to see how this comes together." The first is a negative, while the second applies curiosity and creates growth. If you don't know how to do something you want to do, that's confirmation that discovering how should be part of your goal.

> IF YOU DON'T KNOW HOW TO DO SOMETHING YOU WANT TO DO, THAT'S CONFIRMATION THAT DISCOVERING HOW SHOULD BE PART OF YOUR GOAL.

Motivation is important in setting and adhering to goals. Yes, you will have that negative voice in your head saying, "You don't know how to do this. Give up!" Ignore it. That's just your brain trying to keep you stuck, giving you an excuse not to step out of your comfort zone. Once you're willing to dismiss that as a feeling rather than fact, you'll be back on track again.

Your Action Plan

We've built a strong foundation of belief in where we're headed. We know why we're going there and what it will mean to us once we reach our destination. Now comes the scary part. It's time to create the detailed action plan to get you there. I don't want to simply leave you with motivation and nothing else. Let's make this a reality together.

Grab your notebook again, and write down three concrete goals (or revenue streams you'll create) that will lead you to achieving your ultimate why—your purpose you identified earlier. Start with the end in mind, and work your way backward. What are three concrete goals you can set that will undoubtedly lead you to your purpose? For example, as a business coach, I knew one goal would be having at least ten coaching clients. I also knew creating two paid speaking engagements would take me closer to my why. These became two of my first goals. What are your three specific, measurable goals that will help you reach your why?

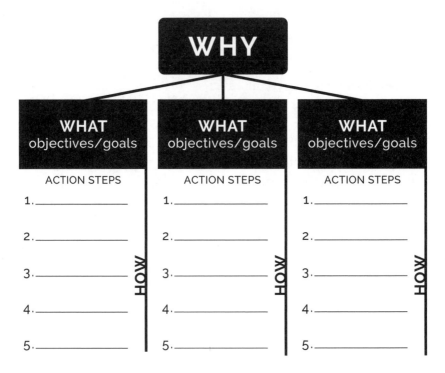

Next, write down what it would mean to you to accomplish those goals. You should be both motivated and a little bit scared by having these goals in writing. When you push past your comfort zone, you will feel uneasy. After all, you're in new territory now. But your uneasiness should be a good feeling, because it's a sign that you're in the zone where growth happens. If you look at those goals and feel fired up and ready to go, good for you! If you don't—if the goals are too daunting and you don't wholeheartedly believe you can achieve them—then adjust them to be more realistic. Now select one of your three concrete goals and write down a manageable, actionable step that would serve as a benchmark on the path to the ultimate goal you selected. A benchmark for me would have been creating a website to use to advertise my coaching process to potential clients or starting an email list to send regular communication to potential clients. Making sense? Think again of a long drive. You know where you'll be ending up, but you need to plan on points you can use to measure your progress in terms of "When I reach this spot, I will be almost halfway there."

Your goals and benchmarks are the backbone of your action plan. Once you have it formulated, you'll suddenly realize you have an action plan for how you'll reach each of your goals and ultimately your why. Having your map of how you'll get to your goals is very helpful, but it's also important that your plan be fluid and flexible.

My best advice is to proceed with curiosity and the assumption that whatever happens along the way will be something that's helpful and leading you toward your highest potential. For example, even if you're driving and are forced to take a detour, the detour will take you somewhere you haven't been, which could be refreshing and interesting; the contented driver lets it add to their enthusiasm and figures it's for the best—after all, she could be avoiding damaging her car on the road that's closed for repairs. She made the assumption in that example that the detour was for her benefit and not to her detriment. As best you can, continue to make the same assumptions about the inevitable detours that will arise on your journey to your goals.

It's also important that your plan remains fluid so you can course-correct as you go along. Every plan ends up needing adjustments, whether you're making a shirt, sailing to Bermuda, or heading toward what you were meant to do. This way you're a lot less likely to panic or lose faith.

When you get to one of your benchmarks, you can reassess your plan. For instance, you might have already reached a goal you thought would take longer, or you could have discovered that you would be wise to learn how to do something that will help you as you continue but that you hadn't planned to learn. That's not a problem. You are still headed in the right direction and chugging along.

Making Your Path Easier

Another important but often skipped-over step in goal setting is making a note of the items that will make the path to your goals easier and more efficient. For instance, what are the resources you will need to accomplish each goal? These will generally fall into three categories: skills, abilities, and actual resources. They can include resources you already have or are currently missing. These can range from basic things like renting office space or an upgraded home office setup to learning a new skill—say, how to create a newsletter or blog—or polishing an existing aptitude, such as your presentation skills. Maybe you need to learn a whole new software program or research how to apply for various licenses or accreditations.

Think carefully while making your list to get the details down. Will you need a van instead of your car? A new accountant? An assistant to handle minor chores, freeing you to take on the heavy-duty work? Next to each item, write down the name of anyone who might be able to help, who is knowledgeable about that area. Let's say you're hoping to get your career as an illustrator going in your spare time. You will need specific things: sample illustrations, which will have to be created if you don't have anything in print; portfolios you can use for storing your work or sending to a magazine if they ask to see one; a cover letter you will need to create; and a list of art directors open to seeing new work. If this is your first goal on the way to working as an illustrator, you already have a list of four actions to get out of the way before you reach the goal of showing your work to art directors.

Make another list of *anyone* who can help you achieve your goals. Use the acronym FRANK—Friends, Relatives, Acquaintances, Neighbors, Kids/Career—and you will soon realize that you know far more people than you thought you did. Think broadly. Look on LinkedIn for old college friends and neighbors you had when growing up, and see what they're up to. As you're searching for resources, don't overlook the obvious or make assumptions about people—just write a broad list, because you never know how the people you know might become important players in your reaching your goals. At the end of this process, you should have a much more organized action plan that still leaves room for changing course.

Keeping Up the Momentum and Your Spirits

One of the keys to reaching your goals is *don't procrastinate*. Procrastination is just another way your mind keeps you stuck. It is merely disguised fear—either the fear of losing something you already have or the fear of not getting what you want. Either way, it's that self-centered fear we talked about earlier. It raises its head again as you try to plug along on your action steps.

It's funny in a way, but we are so frightened of taking action that we become frozen by that fear. Yet what keeps us from accomplishing our goals is our sitting there thinking and not moving. The reality is that you can't think yourself into the right action, but you can act your way into the right thinking!

Don't let yourself get obsessed by the *how*, and stay away from any assumptions stemming from your previous experience that tell you what you *should* be doing. You can do it any way you want. Your past experience—other than the skills you picked up along the way that could now prove valuable—is not relevant anymore. It can often just limit you. Worrying about the "hows" and "shoulds" cuts you off from the moment and blocks forward movement. A little bit of movement in the direction of your dream is better than no movement at all. Avoiding procrastination and keeping your enthusiasm high are the best ways to keep the momentum going into the unknown future.

Stick to Your Plan

Staying away from the "shoulds" and following your vision for your career become difficult when you're offered opportunities you might previously have taken. A perfect example of this "offer you can't refuse" happened to an artist I worked with recently. Together we developed her why so that she could use it as her guidepost for achieving more in the future.

Shortly after, her belief in herself and her why were tested, just as I expect yours will be. She was offered a project designing the covers of a book collection, a great opportunity in product design. The deal would have been extremely lucrative and potentially given her exposure in an exciting new market. The only problem was the project wasn't aligned with her purpose—her why. The work would be time consuming and wasn't taking her any closer to her ultimate vision for her career, which had nothing to do with book jacket design. It would have likely been a detour away from her purpose, but this is exactly the kind of offer people talk themselves into taking. After all, the project would give her both income and prestige. How could she not take it, right?

Her dilemma: follow her intuition and what it was telling her based on her intrinsic values or snap up the opportunity based on fear and a concern about what the rest of the world might say. She kept saying that turning it down felt irresponsible. But I would challenge you to be honest with yourself and consider whether it's irresponsible or just an old habit—a lack of belief in your own intuition. Your strong foundation built on belief in yourself becomes critical when you're offered opportunities like these that will take you away from your dream. You know where you're headed and what you want out of your life. Don't let fear or old habits get in the way of where you're going.

She decided to trust her intuition and turn down the work. She believed in herself and had worked hard to get where she was as an artist, and she had faith that following her dream would pay off. It did! Shortly afterward, she was offered the largest commission of her career thus far for a piece of original artwork. Her commitment to her why paid off, and it will for you too.

I'm not saying there's anything wrong with creating designs for products. Commercial art is a field in which many talented and even famous artists love working. That didn't make it right for her. It would have meant putting her dream on hold indefinitely, and she would have taken it only out of the fear of not being able to achieve her dream or fear of losing income. See that self-centered fear again?

When you stick with what you value, you will steer the course you have set. You will do it with flexibility, changing it when you want to, not when the world tells you to. This doesn't mean that choosing something commercial is wrong, any more than choosing to stick with what you love, even if it means less money, is irresponsible. The world doesn't have to be an either/or place. What matters is following the path that is a right fit for *you* and that makes you the happiest.

> THE WORLD DOESN'T HAVE TO BE AN EITHER/OR PLACE. WHAT MATTERS IS FOLLOWING THE PATH THAT IS A RIGHT FIT FOR YOU AND THAT MAKES YOU THE HAPPIEST.

Self-Motivation Is a Commitment to Your Future

Now that you have your goals and your action plan, you have a map that will continue to show you where you are and where you're headed. I didn't have this firmly in hand when I decided to leave the practice of law or sales coaching. Yes, I was dipping my toe out of **The Loop**, trying something new, but I still wasn't ready to face the reality of who I was, what I really wanted, and how I was going to get there. And while I was good at teaching other women how to build sales careers for themselves, I still had **The Tug** that told me I wasn't where I wanted to be. I had to conquer my own fear and pain before I could become who I wanted to be.

You might have to do that as well, and the next chapter will help guide you. In the meantime, remember that motivation is not just about keeping the excitement going but about continuously choosing the direction that generates even more excitement. It's about adapting your habits to those that will keep you making progress and assure you you're making the right moves. I hope you'll continue to write down your thoughts while you get started with the most doable tasks (oh, yes—you can start before you're done with this book). Make a commitment to stick to your plan and your deadlines. Stay organized and work and believe in yourself every day. Learn what lures you off the path. Take your time, but don't waste it. Do all the above while never forgetting that you have an innate gift and are on the way to letting it fulfill you.

YOUR ROCK MIDDLE REMINDER:

Create a flexible plan, and trust yourself and your intuition. Find confidence and courage in knowing that what you value most is what's right for you.

CHAPTER FIVE

THE PAIN OF STAYING THE SAME

These pains you feel are messengers. Listen to them.

—RUMI

When is the best time to start working on becoming the person you were meant to be? I say do it as soon as you feel unsatisfied with what you're doing. Don't wait like I did. When vague complaints or objections about your daily grind solidify into pain and unhappiness, you owe it to yourself to start making changes. Your subconscious is giving you a gentle push to get your attention. As we've discussed, we stay where we are because we fear the change.

Most people wait to make a change until the pain of staying the same is greater than the potential pain of change. You don't have to do that.

I didn't make a change for years because I was still locked into the old paradigms and beliefs that told me I'd be a fool to give up a six-figure income to risk failure. Over the years, I had inklings I could do something else. I even had an opportunity, but I made my decision the way I always had, with the same fears, beliefs, and habits, using the same stinking thinking. I hadn't changed my belief in myself, so I wasn't capable of having the courage to change my life. I hadn't built my solid foundation yet.

I lived at either end of the spectrum—at zero or at ten—swinging the pendulum between the two ends daily. We all tend to swing the pendulum. At zero it sounds like, "I'm never going to get any more work, so I might as well close my business!" and at ten, "This is it! This is the thing that will make all my dreams come true." Neither end is accurate. That's why living life swinging from end to end is another way of trapping ourselves, of halting our growth and staying stuck.

We need to aim for living with the pendulum at four, five, and six. This is one middle spot that's a wise choice! At four, five, and six, we get to have a little bit of both ends of the pendulum. For example, imagine seeing an aggressive person getting ahead (they operate at ten) and a timid one getting left behind (they're at zero). We convince ourselves that the choice is one or the other—zero or ten, the aggressive person or the timid one. But that's not true. You can compromise and be a bit of both, which is the middle ground, with the pendulum at four, five, and six. Think about this: When was the last time you truly respected someone who didn't like themselves, who either shrank into the background or bullied their way into the spotlight? We tend to respect those that don't live at either end of the pendulum. We respect those that stick to the middle ground.

My Jenga Tower

I lived in extremes, swinging the pendulum back and forth, fearing that any move might be the one that pulled everything in my life apart. My life was built much more like a Jenga tower instead of that strong pyramid with a sturdy foundation. My tower was always shaky and about to fall down. That's one reason Rock Middle was so miserable for me. It might be our comfort zone, but it isn't as cozy as we try to convince ourselves it is.

Something quite small could happen, and I would be a wreck over it. Everything threatened me. If one of my kids got sick or a I got a flat tire, it was like someone pulled a tenuous piece of the tower out of its place, making the entire structure tremble. I would immediately swing to zero, thinking, *My day is ruined!* What I know now is that I hadn't built a life on my beliefs but instead on everyone else's beliefs. So when any aspect of my day broke down, I fell apart. I couldn't handle anything other than throwing myself into my work. My internal message was, *I have sacrificed my happiness for this success. How can my life not be perfect? Why isn't everything coming together?* No wonder I was continually exhausted: trying to ignore what was going on was the hardest work of all.

I made what could have been a good decision, to leave the law firm and start a new career, but because I still hadn't dealt with my belief in who I was, things got worse instead of better. I could no longer tell myself, *If only I weren't a lawyer, I'd be happy.* I quickly believed I was being forced to do something stifling and limiting again, but that was me just swinging to zero. The only common denominator in all of this was me. I couldn't get out of the pain because everywhere I went, there I was. Once I became a full-time entrepreneur, there was much more time to fill up being busy and much more time to feel the pain. I started to feel more of the emotional anguish. It had me crying here and there and saying things like, "I feel frustrated, but I don't know why." I continued to ignore the emotional pain, which after a while turned into physical symptoms. My back and shoulders were constantly aching.

I still considered living at this level of stress and pain to be normal. In fact, in conversation, we all tend to express pride in being both busy and stressed, as if that's shorthand for, "I'm no better than you; we're all in the same boat." It's more socially acceptable to speak to friends about our busyness and stress than to admit how rich, abundant, or joyful our lives are. Even people who are all three of those things have said to me, "I can't tell people that, because it would be bragging!"

I didn't seek support for the pain. I didn't feel as if I could. So I did what I could to escape my own thoughts. I pushed down the emotional and physical suffering. Some people do it with retail therapy, eating, or drugs. I did it with alcohol.

My Pain of Staying the Same

I share this part of my story because I didn't know there could ever be real consequences to my pain. I thought it was just a rite of passage to feel some extraordinary distress. Let me assure you, that's not required. I believed if I were honest about how I felt, others would judge me, and I'd never reach success. I now know I don't need external recognition to reach sincere happiness—which is real success to me. I just need to believe in myself and seek internal fulfillment above all else.

Since I didn't share my distress, I numbed it. That always backfires, because if we're going to create real change, we have to be open and honest about it. This is me being as open, honest, and vulnerable about my own pain as I can be. If sharing this part of my story can help someone else escape the agony faster, then I'm all for it.

I once heard someone say, "The South romanticizes alcohol." Well, I don't know about that, but I had romanticized it for sure. My idea of success included me in a suit with a cocktail in my hand. Drinking was always part of my life. Everything was celebrated with a drink. It never occurred to me it might turn out to be detrimental.

I partied a lot in college, but I never considered it an issue. It didn't get in the way of anything. The same was true when I was practicing law. People drank, and I was one of them. No big deal.

There were certainly some signs I might have paid attention to back then, but nothing adverse occurred. Things weren't great the last few years while I ran the law firm and grew the sales company, but they had been manageable. However, once I walked away from running the law firm, late nights out became a bit more of the norm. I no longer had the accountability of needing to be in an office every morning. I worked from home, and this newfound freedom (or lack of accountability) gave me just the permission slip I needed to ride the elevator all the way to my rock bottom.

I felt sorry for myself. By that point, I had completely stopped believing in myself. I had convinced myself that my big dreams of making an impact on the world weren't feasible anymore. I was sure I'd made the mistake of choosing the wrong career again and was incredulous that I'd repeated past wrongs. I believed I'd never be able to achieve anything bigger than what I had now, so I might as well let go and numb the pain, as it wasn't going anywhere. I had wasted my chances. My dream either was a figment of my imagination or had already passed me by without my realizing it. It was as if I were empty of hope, unable to see beyond Rock Middle at all. I wasn't living by any of the principles I believe in so strongly now—the principles I've been sharing with you that have changed my life.

By that point, I was just performing. I was still reaching sales goals because, no matter what, I had to maintain the outward expression of success. I couldn't let that go. If I could just keep up the show on the outside, then no one would find out just how much pain I was in on the inside. But it didn't matter what I felt like on the inside. I desperately needed to keep up appearances rather than be discovered as the imposter I felt I was.

I felt like a terrible fraud, which only made the disconnect between my internal and external self grow. There I was—smiling, selling, and sad—as I taught women how to sell more product. More and more, I was crying a lot, but only in private. I tried so many different experiments within the job in an attempt to be happy: cutting back in one area, spending more time in another. I had already sought help with therapists, but they weren't making a difference. Maybe it was because I wasn't being honest with myself or them. However, I was so lost that I couldn't see the real cause of my unhappiness.

In the meantime, I had a big sales event planned with my twin sister. We had done this event together for years, and it had always been lucrative. That year, I wasn't prepared. I had reached the point where even the external didn't matter to me anymore. I was in so much emotional and physical pain by then that I could barely muster up the energy to work. How did I handle it? Every night of that event, I went out and got drunk. I just couldn't face the current reality of things. The business I'd built in sales wasn't where I wanted it to be anymore, and I thought I once again had no choice but to grin and bear it. I had to find a way to escape.

The last night turned out to be the one that changed everything. I overslept and was late picking up my son from camp. I'll never forget this day. He had a huge smile on his face when I arrived. He didn't care that I was late. He loved me anyway. He loved me just the way I was. I saw myself through his eyes for a minute, and it was a feeling I hadn't let myself feel in so long, that genuine love and connection. He didn't care what I achieved or did for a living. He just loved me. I took a picture of us at that moment. To this day, it's one of the pictures I treasure most.

We had a long drive back home, more than six hours, and I spent most of it in tears. When I got home, I looked at myself in the mirror, at the mess I had become. I didn't recognize the person in the reflection. How had I gotten so far off my path? I went to see my therapist the next day. She said I had been talking to her about alcohol being an issue throughout the last year. Needless to say, I had no recollection of that. It was if my subconscious had been speaking to her while I was somewhere else. See, once we let down the walls, I believe we begin to see all of the things that were there waiting for us all along: all of the people who can help, all of the resources we have sitting in front of us. We just can't see them until we're ready to let down those walls and get honest about where we are in our lives.

The day after that, I had a meeting set up with a friend I intended to collaborate with on a speech, a friend who just so happened to be in recovery. She walked in and said, "Ready to work on the speech?"

My answer was, "I think I have a drinking problem."

She just laughed and said, "Okay, great. That will be easy to solve. Right now, I'm much more concerned about how this speech is going to sound." Even through my tears, I started laughing. That evening I started my journey to get sober, and I've never looked back since. I finally let go. I let go of what others would think of me. I let go of my attempts to control every aspect of my life. The thought that I ever had the power to control everything seems comical to me now. I let go of the internal judgment of myself long enough to say, "I want a better life than the one I'm living now."

I believe those were the steps meant for me. They were the ones I had to experience to move forward and let go. You've likely faced setbacks in your life, and now, hopefully, you can see them as steps forward instead of backward. The way those days and events came together felt like divine intervention. In my gut, I knew this was my chance to get out of pain. Not that I wanted to do it. That's normal too. We hesitate when it comes to change, because we're scared of what the new reality will look like. But I knew I had come to a fork in the road, and this was going to be the better way.

That was the beginning of the hardest year of my life. I had to reverse the order of everything. I had to figure out who I was and what I believed before I could ever figure out what I was meant to do. I had no idea who I was without having someone else tell me. I spent an enormous amount of time focusing on my own growth; that became my number one job, even though I was still working. As much as I wondered where I was going to go from there and where I was going to end up, I didn't force it. I needed a break from all the pushing, whether it was hustling for more income or pushing away my unhappiness. I had to trust that I would know when the moment was right to take my next step toward professional growth.

You will too. You'll know when the moment is right for you to make a choice toward bigger growth, but in the meantime, focus on yourself until the moment is right. You deserve the time to focus on you and to take a breath and focus inside yourself instead of outside. It may take a little time, and I know (believe me) that can be the last thing you want to give the time to, but here's what I have learned: you'll have to do it now or later.

Taking you back to the Jenga tower I mentioned earlier, my life once felt like a narrow tower, and when one peg came out, I would topple over. That's because I didn't have a firm foundation. I hadn't taken this time to build my life, business, or career on a sturdy, wide base. I believe the firm foundation comes from a strong internal belief in who you are and where you're headed. When you know both of these things, there's little the outside world can do to shake you, to topple your tower, because you're built much more like a pyramid. You know trials and tribulations will come, but they won't knock you down every time a peg is removed. You'll simply adjust as life comes at you.

Ditch "Fine" for "Fantastic"

Not everyone hits Rock Middle with the force I did or has to ride the elevator all the way down, but most people who find themselves in Rock Middle find themselves in pain. And all the time, they're telling people they're fine. Sure, as in "F**ked up, Insecure, Neurotic, and Emotional." They might even believe they're fine—other than the little detail that they're totally miserable.

One woman came to me after she found herself having her own bathroom floor moment. She was on the floor crying and not knowing what was wrong. It was her husband who showed her a post of mine on Facebook and said, "Maybe she can help." He had no idea what to do to help. She was miserable and had no idea why. She was in the pain of staying the same.

For over a decade, she had held the same position, with little pressure to perform at a higher level. She wasn't being challenged to grow in any aspect of her life. Like many women stuck in their careers, she had a tremendous amount of guilt about her feelings of frustration. She felt guilty that she wasn't satisfied with the status quo. She had it all—the white picket fence, three kids, and a loving husband. How could she possibly feel frustrated? She didn't want to admit her pain to anyone else. In fact, she agreed to meet with me only because she felt guilty about the strain she was putting on her marriage and friendships.

At first, she was the epitome of everything being "fine." I mean, to the point where we almost had to do battle over her consistent use of the word. Finally, she admitted she was not fine. Identifying her dream was the first step, but she felt too much fear and guilt to consider actually taking action on it. She was terribly afraid of coming out of her **Box**, where everything was "fine." She was concerned about the ramifications it would have on her marriage, her kids, her current job. If there was someone else to focus on and think about before herself, she was absolutely going to do that.

None of this is unusual. You see, we're thinking about the unknown and all we'll lose, our comfort and consistency, but we never think about what we stand to gain by making a change. If we consider what we could gain, then we might realize what we'd be losing if we choose to stay the same. Maybe then more people would make the harder choice to choose change. Many people try to avoid making a choice altogether. People often think that if they stay where they are, they aren't really choosing anything but just allowing life to come at them organically as it should. A long time ago, I had a client say, "I'm going to wait and see what happens." But as I told her, that's simply not how it works. Even you saying you'll see represents you making a choice; nothing just happens. It all results from our choices. You can't brush off being a participant by saying, *If it's meant to be, it will happen.* You have to be an active contributor to your own life and future.

> YOU HAVE TO BE AN ACTIVE CONTRIBUTOR TO YOUR OWN LIFE AND FUTURE.

Once my client started to be a participant again and realized she had choices she could make, she started sharing her dream with me, her passion for art and desire to be involved in the art world. We took it slowly. Again, you don't need to make an overnight change to escape Rock Middle. Slow and steady does win the race when you're building a new life on a new foundation. She volunteered at a gallery to start, and after that, she began slowly creating her business as an art consultant. She helped clients choose art, took them to galleries, and worked with them to best display art they already owned or to choose new pieces.

Her dream quickly became a genuine business. She is now dividing her time between the two careers, making the transition gradually. The pain begins to subside once you make the move toward happiness, and everything in your life benefits. Her existing job improved, because as her self-confidence grew, so did her sales. Now that she has an action plan upon which to build her future, she's happier than ever. Fine is no longer good enough for her.

How I Walked Away from My Bag of Rocks

A client recently said, "I didn't realize I was carrying this fifty-pound bag of rocks with me everywhere. Now that I've put them down and begun to dream again, everything in my life feels lighter." Nothing feels as light as the excitement of possibilities to come.

As soon as you commit to taking the first step in your action plan, a load will be lifted from your shoulders too. You may still have fears and doubts, but they will now feel like a shrinking bag of pebbles, not a burdensome sack of rocks. Transitioning gradually into your chosen career will allow you to gain more knowledge in a new area, hone your skills, and give you the comfort of knowing you can stop if you choose. I'm betting you won't, but just in case, it's comforting to know you can. Plus it's smart to continue receiving income from one career while you build up an acceptable cash flow in the other. Your contacts in career number one could also become your clients in career number two. That's a nice bonus.

Some people are happiest having more than one area of work and can do this successfully for their entire lives. Think of all those advertising agency executives, editors, and government professionals who also write novels, for example. They find the time to do both because they love their work.

I was making my transition gradually, feeling sure that I'd found my dream career in business coaching, but I still wasn't ready to let go of my security blanket—my sales career. I wasn't ready to move on quite yet. How could I be sure this time I had gotten it right?

I threw myself wholeheartedly into sales and coaching for six absolutely miserable weeks. I had to give it one last shot. I wanted to know if I would feel as though I was expanding into who I wanted to become or shrinking into the old person I was ready to leave behind. We each have a different path to knowing when to walk away. There's no one size fits all, but I can say that the best thing you can do is evaluate whether your path is helping you continue to expand or if it feels genuinely constricting. When you really get in touch with yourself, you'll know if you're ready to walk away or give it one last shot.

When you have outgrown who you were and you attempt to go backward, it feels as if you're putting on your pre-baby skinny jeans (ha!). It's tight, uncomfortable, and you're shocked that the old you ever fit in the first place. Sales coaching wasn't where my heart and soul wanted me to be anymore. Once I let the truth out, I couldn't stuff it back in. Trying to force myself back into that confining container didn't work. It brought up all the pain again. It was finally clear to me that I couldn't stay in the same place. I needed to find a bigger container for myself, the place where I was meant to be. I was now prepared to take the steps, putting one foot in front of the other, to change everything. I wasn't going to put pressure on myself. I no longer needed to feel busy and miserable. The joy of knowing who I was and where I was going erased that need. I was free.

Once you've made up your mind to do work you feel passionately about, you'll feel the freedom you desire. Feeling that freedom is possible at any age or stage of your life. You'll always have things that could hold you back—the usual excuses, debt, kids, mortgage—but as Marie Forleo likes to say, "Everything is figureoutable!"

I can't say I wish I had taken steps sooner. Yes, I could have saved myself a great deal of misery, but that wasn't in the cards for me. If I had tried full force sooner, I don't think I would have been ready. I was so locked into my role, into my title, that I don't think I could have succeeded—the potential pain of change was simply too great at the time to push harder.

We change when we are ready. We seek help when we both know and admit we need it. It simply takes what it takes, and that will be different for each person. And then we proceed, perhaps with a bit of trepidation, but at least no longer with the pain that makes us drop to the bathroom floor in misery. I could be the poster girl for staying stuck in Rock Middle, and I got out. I'm confident you can do it too.

You Don't Need to Suffer Intensely to Grow

I chose to share my own story and that of my client as examples of how deep the pain of staying the same helped cause us to hit Rock Middle in our own way. But I don't want you to think that you need your own bathroom floor moment in order to have hit Rock Middle. For example, I have a client who has her own successful public relations company. She loves what she's doing, but she wanted to feel the joy that comes from moving even closer to your greatest potential. She felt **The Tug** despite being very satisfied with her career. She didn't need or want an extensive career change. She chose to follow her **Tug** and is currently creating an online education company to help small-business owners with public relations. Her choice was to take her life and career to a higher level. Had she chosen to stay in her current position and give up on her **Tug** for more, she would have been choosing to remain in Rock Middle.

Hitting Rock Middle doesn't have to mean that you're desperately unhappy. It is more that you're not doing what you know deep down inside would make you realize your full potential. Yes, most people are somewhere between miserable and dissatisfied when they have hit Rock Middle, but the change they choose to make to get out of it can be subtle or extreme.

One vital lesson I've learned about what happens to people once they make the move to get out of Rock Middle is that they may choose to do more than one thing. Why shouldn't they? We are all multifaceted and have more than a single interest. Some of us are our best selves concentrating on our main passion, while others discover that what makes them happiest is experimenting with several opportunities. You can create a career that isn't like anyone else's. Just because it doesn't exist yet doesn't mean you can't make it yours.

> YOU CAN CREATE A CAREER THAT ISN'T LIKE ANYONE ELSE'S. JUST BECAUSE IT DOESN'T EXIST YET DOESN'T MEAN YOU CAN'T MAKE IT YOURS.

I have a friend who used to be a college professor. Now she is a writer and a baker—and she's also a marathon runner. She makes a full-time living with her baking and writing, which affords her the ability to travel and run marathons. Just because you don't see someone else who has the same mix of careers that you feel passionate about doesn't mean you can't make that mix work for you. Once we break free of the "shoulds," we are free to invent any career or combination of careers we'd most like to have.

The pain, boredom, or feelings of being stifled or not truly yourself come from staying the same. There are no rules about what you should or shouldn't do or how to do it. Yes, growth is also painful, but like the physical growing pains we experience as children, growth pains tell you that you too are moving in the right direction into a future of independence and satisfaction.

YOUR ROCK MIDDLE REMINDER:

It takes courage to change and grow, but when the time comes, a weight will be lifted from you as you embrace the incredible possibilities of the future.

CHAPTER SIX

TAKE THE NEXT STEP

Authenticity is the process and practice of allowing
the unfolding of the deeper essence of our true
nature to rise to the surface of our lives.

—HEATHER WHITE

I f you have already started with the first step toward your first
three goals, good for you! If not, take a deep breath, put one foot
in front of the other, and do it. Pick up the phone, buy some
supplies, start researching, make a list, and share it with someone. Just
take that first step, however minor it may be. The famous quotation
by sixth-century Chinese philosopher Lao Tzu is truly one of the best
uses of eleven words ever: "The journey of a thousand miles begins
with a single step." Once you give yourself that big push to begin,
you are on the path. Now your task is to show up and keep moving.

Once you cultivate the awareness of what you want and can see
that there's more on the horizon, you can't go back to where you were
and be the same person. You can't lose the awareness once you have
it. The old path is now an illusion. It simply doesn't exist. It disap-
peared forever once you gained awareness, because you're a different
person now. My daughter gave me a perfect, concrete example of this

recently. She has always kept her favorite pajamas from when she was two. Every once in a while, as if she's never tried it before, she decides to put them on, telling me, "I'll bet I can still get into them."

When she said this the last time, I responded, "Yes, you can put them on your body, but they can't possibly fit you anymore. The pants will be up to your knees, the short sleeves will be jammed into your armpits, and while they will be on your body, they won't fit."

My point is this: you can try to go back, but you've outgrown that place in the same way she's outgrown her PJs. And the more she grows, the smaller and tighter they'll feel, just like your old comfort zone. You'll actually feel more comfortable once you gain acceptance with the steps you take to move forward. Don't worry. It's an old habit for most of us to want to go backward. Growth is hard work and awkward. It's natural to occasionally long to shake off your awareness and get back into your old comfort zone. The good news is that you will be creating a new comfort zone. It will just be bigger than the one you once had.

Many people encouraged me to leave my comfort zone before by showing me the image below, suggesting that as soon as you leave your "comfort zone," you get to jump to the other circle that says, "This is where the magic happens." I disagree. I always want to draw my own circle in the gap between the two circles and write, "This is where the discomfort happens." We don't skip blithely from the comfort zone to the magic. I wish we did, but it's just not like that. I believe we too often make people think it's that simple or feels good when they're on their way to where they're meant to be. Who says? Having been someone who walked the journey from one circle to the next, I can tell you it isn't that simple, and it tends to not always feel great.

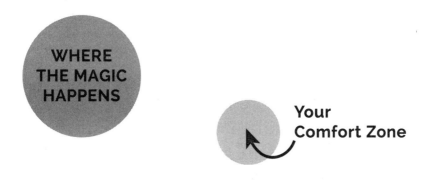

This is the reality of it:

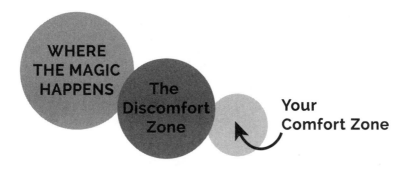

Growth can feel strange and uncomfortable at times. Have you ever had to learn a new sport as an adult? I have! I've been the only forty-year-old on the bunny slopes with the four-year-olds. Let me tell you, it was uncomfortable and rather embarrassing. When other people asked me if I knew what I was doing, I wanted to ditch and run, but I knew the only way to get better was to endure the discomfort. The gap between your current comfort zone and "where the magic happens" will be filled with moments of discomfort and maybe even a few embarrassments, too.

You wouldn't let me ditch my ski school class of four- and five-year-olds, so I'm not going to let you come this far with awareness, knowledge, and steps outside your comfort zone only to have you ditch it now because of a little discomfort. Expect the discomfort. Look forward to it and laugh when it arrives, and if you need a little help, picture me as the only adult getting passed on the bunny slope by kids the height of my kneecaps.

Change is a process. We want to progress toward our dream, not perfection. It's not supposed to feel really awesome all at once. When we're outside our comfort zone, feeling the discomfort and learning to walk through it, we are making that progress. Ultimately, you can feel at ease knowing that the discomfort on the journey serves an important purpose. It helps you learn the lessons you'll need to know once you reach your destination.

On Cloud Nine

Once I got up the gumption to make the change, I was all in for it. Knowing my destination was becoming a business coach, I did what I've suggested you do.

I made a list of what I needed to do—just the first few steps so I wouldn't get too overwhelmed with all that had to be done to reach the destination. I set three small goals. They were:

1. Develop a structure for one-on-one coaching for clients.

2. Create a company name and email address.

3. Find someone to create a logo and business cards.

These things made me feel like I was in business. I was very quiet as I took those first steps. I made no announcements, told no one.

I didn't even tell anyone when I followed my intuition and snuck away to Kentucky to attend a conference for new entrepreneurs. I was excited and curious as could be. I told myself, *Okay, I'm only exploring opportunities and not making any decisions. I'm following my intuition, and my intuition is telling me to go.* So I headed to Kentucky to spend forty-eight hours to explore what was next. That trip was exactly the next step I needed, and I'm grateful to this day that I listened to my intuition and went.

My advice to you is to go for it too. Follow your intuition, and do whatever you can to let yourself discover what it would be like to explore your dream. I wanted to see how it would feel, expansive or constricting. It turned out to be the best thing ever to give myself the space to explore moving forward and sit in those feelings. It was like trying on a dress for size and seeing if it makes you feel good or doesn't. I went to that conference in my new dress, which was my new identity. When people asked me what I did, I said, "I'm a business coach." It was the first time I had ever uttered those words out loud. It felt amazing! It felt freeing, and for the first time in years, I saw my life filled with possibilities. It was as if I had been driving through fog, and suddenly it cleared to reveal the road ahead as exciting and promising. I knew in a flash that coaching was where I needed and wanted to be.

I came back from that trip brimming with enthusiasm, and that's when I started to take more formal steps toward establishing my company. I thought it would take a year to make the transition, and I was fine with that. Instead, it took a month, just one month. I was so ready. For me, the light was on, and everything looked bright. *Oh, my gosh*, I thought, *I see where I'm supposed to be now!* It all fell into place: what my purpose was, why I'd had to go through everything I had, and why I'd learned what I learned. Now I could see how each thing was going to come into play to help other people.

As I started moving forward enthusiastically, I felt overwhelmed. For me, frustration comes hot on the heels of feeling overwhelmed. This time was no exception. Thinking about how much had to be done to create the business and company I wanted made me quickly fall back into old patterns of stinking thinking, with self-messaging like "This will take forever. I'll never get where I really want to go." I had fallen into the other side of **The Expertise Trap**—believing I had to research and know it *all* before I got started. That's simply not true either. Remember? "There are people out there doing exactly what it is that you want to do right now, with less expertise and less talent than you have, and they're making millions of dollars doing it." Don't fall prey to trying to know it all before you get started, or you'll never start.

Is it even possible for you to actually know it all, anyway? I'll answer that for you in case you hesitate. No. It's not possible. You'll never reach a point where you say, "Ah, that's it. I officially know it all." Right? Right! Because knowledge and information are two things you can always count on changing. You're setting yourself up for a self-defeating, losing battle, so let go of that idea and get started.

A good rule of thumb is to follow the production-versus-consumption rule. For every hour you spend consuming (reading, watching, listening), you should spend at least four hours producing. This means if you're like me and want to be the foremost expert before you begin, you need fewer courses, fewer masterminds, fewer trainings, and fewer webinars. This is critical to making progress. We can't just stop everything and drown ourselves in research. If we spend all of our time consuming information without acting on it, we're not going to get closer to our dream. We'll just achieve a temporary feeling of expertise that is strictly theoretical.

I have a Post-it Note in my office that I will never take down. It helped me so many times through the initial period of discomfort when I believed I should "learn it all, do it all" before I got started. It simply says, "Next Step." It's a reminder to me that the only step I can take is the next one, so there's no need to worry about more than that. I simply take the next step in front of me and trust the rest will come. Keep moving, and don't put pressure on yourself and overextend. You don't need to do twenty steps today. Or tomorrow. You just need to keep moving step by step and not let yourself get trapped in the discomfort. Having that reminder when I was starting out helped daily. The only things we can control are our actions today.

> THE ONLY THINGS WE CAN CONTROL ARE OUR ACTIONS TODAY.

You don't have to follow my Post-it Note suggestion; just find something that works for you. You see, the fear grows when we live in the land of the unknown. Since the future is largely unknown, it's inevitable that our fear grows when we spend so much time consumed with it. Trying to project too far ahead does that. But when you're thinking about the next step, you aren't in the future; you're in today. I try to live where my feet are planted at the moment. When I get overwhelmed, I look down and remind myself, I'm right here. My feet are on the floor underneath this chair where I'm sitting. That reminds me to get back into the present moment and do the only thing I can reasonably do at that time: take the next step and have faith that the rest will unfold as it's intended. When you can pull yourself back into the present moment, you are moving out of a state of fear and back into action.

That faith and trust, whether it's faith in yourself or God or the universe, is critical. You need to keep believing that you wouldn't be doing any of this if it weren't meant for you. That's what brought you here to this place of change, isn't it? You were driven by your feeling deep inside that you were meant to do more or achieve something else or change careers. That intuition was so strong because it was meant for you. So whenever you find yourself dwelling on something five steps ahead, that's when you need to disconnect from the future, get back to the present, and start taking your steps one by one. You can always take one step to move you closer to your goals.

Some days, one step will be all you can do, and that's okay. You'll return an email, book a class, check out where to buy something you will need. Maybe you'll sign up with Square, Venmo, or another payment app. Let every step you take inspire you to create further actions. If they don't? Guess what? You can pack up for the day. You're done. Give yourself a break. You have taken a step, which is good. And if you don't really feel great about taking the next one that day, it's time for some self-care. Maybe tomorrow you will take two steps. Maybe not. You are still moving in the right direction. You're walking on sunshine now. You don't need to run.

Inspired Action Comes from Self-Care

As driven, self-motivated women, it's so easy for us to fall into the trap of the hustle, especially when we feel like we're finally moving closer to the life we've always wanted. Society and our inner critic tell us that in order to succeed, we have to push harder and work longer than everyone around us. I used to think that if I stopped hustling, I would fall behind, and the dream I wanted would start to slip through my fingers. Or worse—I'd be considered lazy. Gasp!

However, when I pushed myself too hard, I ran out of energy. I would stop spending time on things that I considered a luxury— yoga, hanging with friends, dates with my husband, all the stuff that actually nourishes me, all my self-care options that we already know are so important. But when I let go of those things, I wasn't recharging myself. The type of energy I would cultivate was more of that tired, negative energy. It became an endless cycle of staying stuck in the exhaustion until I could interrupt it again by taking myself to yoga or making myself sit down and relax.

I want to work in a state of creativity, and in order to do that, I have to take care of me. Self-care is something I never prioritized because I never made the connection between self-care and productivity. As always, I considered it selfish to put myself first. What I've come to learn now is that nothing else works well unless I do. If I'm a mess, then most other things in my life become messy too. It has a trickle-down effect. I cannot create inspired things unless I've taken the time to be inspired too.

So what does inspired action look like? It means I'm in the flow of creativity and passion in a way that makes the work feel easier and less forced. For me, it now means I stop working when I'm uninspired. I take a break when I'm exhausted. I stop going to events that don't fill my cup or my soul. Fundamentally, I stop hustling and shift my mind-set to understand that I won't gain anything by burning myself out. Take a moment to look at your life and calendar, and think about whether you plan to work at times of inspired action or if you've been just forcing yourself to hustle. Examine just how productive you have been in those times when you've tried to grind it out versus the times when you've been inspired. Try to remember how different the two feelings made the work feel. Then commit to cultivating more inspired action and a lot less hustle.

Visualize Your Future

We've created your plan chapter by chapter, starting with the end in mind. That was intentional. It's another critical technique I've found that makes all the difference in making your dream come to life.

Starting with your vision of what you want your life to ultimately look and feel like is the best way to ensure you reach your exact destination. Otherwise, it's too easy to fall into doing a bunch of things with your fingers crossed in the hopes that those things will lead where you want. The result of that approach is, too often, getting that feeling of, *Oh, my gosh, I'm throwing spaghetti on the wall trying a bunch of different things, and I don't even know if any of these things are the right things.* That opens the door to fear and disillusionment.

So knowing I wanted to be a speaker and a business coach, I knew in the end I'd be on stage sharing challenging ideas and working with clients one on one. Then I thought about what specific pieces of my business needed to be in place to support those end goals. My to-do list didn't include what I *should* do. I didn't even think in those terms. It just included those steps necessary to make what I envisioned a reality.

I discourage clients from spending too much time researching what their business should be or look like. After all, if you follow the examples of others when setting up your new career, what will happen to the uniqueness that you want to bring to your endeavor? What will make it quintessentially you? It's your dream, and it should be built according to your vision, what you see yourself doing when you close your eyes. If you do it in the reverse, allowing Google or random websites to tell you what you should do, you risk creating something derivative, something that looks like what everyone else is doing. And that's what I would hate for you to do. Why? Because if you follow someone else's version of a dream career, you will just create another version of **The Loop** by not following your own dream.

I'm not suggesting that you swing the pendulum to ten and never ever do any research or check out others in your industry. But it's important to develop your own vision first. When you need guidance on setting up an LLC or buying a URL, that's the time to go online. But that's not the same as turning to the web to seek out what your company *should* look like.

After you've taken your first few steps, you have to take a deep breath and do something that terrifies you, which is to share your secret. There's a wonderful children's book by Bernard Waber called *Courage*, with a cover illustration of a little boy standing at the end of a diving board. That picture has always stuck with me, because it reminds me that I've faced moments from my childhood on when I needed courage, and I've survived them. To me there's nothing more courageous than sharing your dream with others. I reached the point—as you will, too—where I was standing at the end of a virtual diving board, and I had to dive into the water. In order to succeed, we have to put ourselves out there, right?

You need to tell others you exist, and that's pretty darned scary, because it's like showing your baby to the world and asking for feedback. It might be the first time you have ever exposed your authentic self. We've all spent a lot of time hiding who we really are and pretending to be happy when we weren't. The prospect of taking off the mask will be scary. You are going to show everyone what you wanted most of all, and that's terrifying. But here is where I'll say you need to take the leap.

You can't merely fall off the edge of the board. I want you to do a running cannonball off of it, as big as you possibly can, and announce yourself with pride and confidence. Share the joy and happiness you have found in pursuing the thing you were meant to do. Remember, no one will have more enthusiasm for your business than you do, so set the bar high. Confidence and enthusiasm are the two biggest attracters of others to your business, so don't skimp on either of them.

Whom Do You Want to Serve?

Whether you are making a huge switch, becoming an entrepreneur, or just wishing to take what you're already doing to a whole new level, having a well-defined audience will help you do everything from developing an elevator pitch to writing your website copy. Defining your audience can be one of the keys to success now that you understand your purpose. I suggest identifying the smallest audience to start out with, because what you want are raving fans. With just a few people who think you're the answer to their prayers, your career will be off to a great start. Why? Because they'll praise you—to prospects and potential clients, and even to your coworkers if you're making a corporate move.

One reason I'm so big on starting with the end in mind is that it will save you a lot of time you might have wasted targeting the wrong audience. Take the printing executive whose passion is for painting. His chosen focus is landscapes, large ones. When he envisioned himself marketing large landscapes, he realized that the biggest market for any large works of art was corporate. It's developers and industries that need large works for their walls; after all, most people don't buy full-wall landscapes. So that was another step ahead for him: researching the prices and measurements for large artworks for equally large offices and buildings. If he had worked from the beginning, he could have ended up with a portfolio of works too small for most corporate needs.

Once you have the parameters of your dream in place, you can do all the online research you need in order to refine your audience. My motto is always "look for the white space," which means seek specialized areas that aren't already covered heavily by your competition. It's better to start small, in an area you can call your own. You don't need to concentrate on being a niche provider, but simply aim to discover an area in which you can fulfill your dream and be unique.

Anne Block is a great example. A former actress who was working but not making it big, Anne started with the end in mind too. She knew she cared more about exploring Los Angeles and the rest of the world than acting. In an effort to accomplish her dream, she created a successful specialized tour business. She knew what she loved, and she looked for a need in the market that she could fulfill. She became an individual tour guide to the stars. In fact, Anne's first client was Lily Tomlin. Right after the fall of the Berlin Wall, Tomlin hired Anne to come along for the Berlin Film Festival and show her the city in depth during her free time. Since that private tour, Anne has continued to expand her company on both a national and international level, with specialty tours and a long roster of private and corporate clients for whom her company, Take My Mother, Please, designs individual tours anywhere in the world.

That's what working from the end backward allows you to do: take your dream—in this case, traveling all over the world—and find the white space that makes what you have to offer unique. Then start slowly and build from there. Anne went from showing Lily Tomlin the sights in Berlin to concentrating on driving clients around Los Angeles to expanding gradually into Europe and from Europe to the rest of the world. She took those first steps—and then just kept going. Anne was able to put her acting days behind her to live her dream and prosper as she never had before.

No matter what you choose to do, it's important to base your steps and goals on the fact that the most important thing you have to offer is yourself: your translatable skills, your passion, your determination. As long as you're making your decisions intrinsically, based on your values and who you are and want to be rather than on what others have done, you are on the right path.

There are so many examples of women who are thriving in the business world today because they followed their unique desires and created a market previously unknown. Sara Blakely is a perfect example of that and an inspiration for us all. She pursued her path with a passion that resulted in *Forbes* naming her the world's youngest self-made female billionaire in 2012. No wonder her motto is "Trust your gut"! She started her career selling fax machines door to door. She had tried to become a lawyer before failing the LSAT twice put an end to that. Most people would have settled in a Rock Middle by this point, no longer believing they were meant for extraordinary things. Ask yourself if you would have stopped striving for more at that point.

Blakely didn't stop. Big on visualizing, she had always pictured herself designing a product people needed, even if they didn't know it. She had absorbed the most important lesson her father taught his children: that failure wasn't a question of not achieving something but a matter of not trying. Sara put her heart and soul into anything she did and stayed curious about how her big opportunity would arise. Who would have thought it would come while dressing for a party? Disliking the way a pair of white pants looked on her, she decided they needed a smoother fit. At a loss, she took a pair of control-top pantyhose she had in a drawer and, because she was wearing sandals, cut the feet off of them—and *voilà*!

Sara trusted her intuition and her curiosity about the needs of the market, just like Jen Rubio of Away luggage. She was sure she had a winner, but she had no idea what to do about it. She never let that stop her. She knew the real failure would be *not* trying to market her idea, and that, even though she lacked experience and extensive finances, she had the winning attribute: she cared the most.

Here's a rough summary of Sara's startup steps, based on her *Forbes* interview in March 2019.

Once she cut the feet off those pantyhose, she didn't look back.

1. She bought a book from Amazon on how to create your own patent.

2. She made a very rough prototype held together with tape.

3. She did research on possible manufacturers and pitched until she found the right one.

4. She next pitched to a buyer at Neiman Marcus—and she pitched hard, even taking the other woman into the restroom to show her how well Spanx worked.

5. Once she had the business up and running, she started adding staff. She told *Forbes* she thinks it's important to "hire your weaknesses," which is excellent advice. When you hire people to do what you can do better, you're wasting resources.

Sara did the same thing I did myself in that she told no one what she was doing for a whole year. Note how she took her time and turned her dream into reality one step at a time. You can do the same.

Define Your Worth

No matter what you're doing, know that your unique skills are valuable, and by that, I mean others will pay you money in exchange for your skills and knowledge because it will add monetary value to their company. I have seen too many women defeat themselves by undercharging for their own work due to a fear that no one else would value it. This is one more way to stay stuck and never reach your dream destination. We overperform and undercharge, believing it will one day pay off and take us where we want to go. It won't. You must believe in the value of your work and then set the price point to reflect your belief. Make sure the price is high enough to eventually lead you to your destination.

Ask yourself how much you want to earn. Research, then make a timeline representing the spectrum of potential earnings in your profession. What does someone with your expertise charge? What about the best of the best? What's the top of the market? What's the bottom of the market? Do you see the white space? Funny, but I realized only recently that if I had done this with the practice of law, I probably never would have gotten started. My research would have revealed that top attorneys working their butts off in Manhattan with sixteen years of partnership were making $450,000. That's the top of the market. But of course, I wasn't going to be practicing in New York City, so I would have had to fill in a realistic top of the market for where I was living and ask myself, "Does this match where I actually want to go with my life and my career? Or do I want my earning capabilities to exceed this?" The answer would have been no, it didn't match my desires. I would have realized I didn't want to spend the next decade or more working in a profession that had a capped earning potential.

I recommend this for corporate jobs as well, and it's wise action to take, because while the salary for, let's say, a VP position might be acceptable, research might show you that moving up the ladder from VP to president to CEO or COO in that sector won't bring proportionate compensation, in which case you might want to look for different opportunities—similar specialty career opportunities that would offer better potential income. In the next chapter, I'll talk about going out into the world to build your brand, but the main point here is to know your own worth and charge accordingly. Then you have to believe in yourself and know, as Sara Blakely did, that you have an advantage. Your ace in the hole? No one else in the world can provide the exact same unique set of skills in the way you do.

> YOUR ACE IN THE HOLE? NO ONE ELSE IN THE WORLD CAN PROVIDE THE EXACT SAME UNIQUE SET OF SKILLS IN THE WAY YOU DO.

A Little Hard Truth

As you embark on your first steps, know that not everyone will agree with the move you're making. It's terrible to even consider, but it happens, especially if your dream involves giving up something others deem valuable, like a big salary, comfort, and so on. Friends and colleagues can find it threatening when someone makes a change, especially if they feel, consciously or unconsciously, that it belittles their own choices. That might be the furthest thing from your mind, but it's a fact of life that one person walking away from others' idea of success can strike those people as an assault on what *they're* doing with their lives. When you're already successful, it can be even harder for you, because it will feel as if friends think your happiness should be secondary to your income.

I feel as though I'd be doing you a disservice if I didn't warn you of this, because it can be something that throws people off their path right after they get started. I still often hear, "I can't believe you left the law. Why in the world would you leave all that behind? Don't you regret it?" So I want to prepare you for the time when your friends hear of your plans and warn you against taking action. You might catch friction from those in your innermost circle, those you expect to be the happiest for you. It's not about you, though. It's about them, because anything that upsets the status quo and foretells change is perceived as an assault on their way of life, so they can't get past how your actions will impact them. It will rock the boat for some, and they might try to dissuade you.

Usually, these people come at us in an altruistic manner. They aren't conscious of anything other than wanting what's best for you. They often say things like, "Are you sure that's a good idea?" or "Oh, my gosh, that sounds like it would be so hard!" Most of them are genuinely being protective and want to make sure you have considered the consequences. Remember, other people's brains don't like change, either; they like us to stay in the comfort zone and are scared for us when we step out of it. But it's okay, and unless you think the person is truly coming from a passive-aggressive place, it is well meant. Your courage to continue to follow your own path will encourage others around you to eventually find theirs too. And one day, if they're lucky, they will go off on their own journey just as you're doing.

YOUR ROCK MIDDLE REMINDER:

Follow your path one step at a time, secure in having defined your audience and knowing your own value.

CHAPTER SEVEN

SUCCESS IS AN
ONGOING JOURNEY

People respond well to those that are sure of what they want.

—ANNA WINTOUR

N
ow, let's get into the business of being bigger. I've always been a disbeliever in the idea that when starting out, you had better take whatever work is offered to you. What's the point in going through all this growth if you have to turn around and give your power back to someone else? You don't have to do it that way. I hope that by now you see a pattern here. You can create whatever it is you desire without accepting every bit of work offered. In fact, I believe in the opposite. You've done all of this work to discover yourself, to show up authentically, and to define your audience—now is the time to be clearer than ever about the work you do and the type of client you're eager to serve. Imagine yourself working with that ideal client. Visualize their attributes and what makes them ideal. Then put this message out into the world of who it is you're here to serve, and you will attract those who are a fit with you.

The goal is to create a win-win customer-and-client relationship.

By win-win, I mean both parties get their desired needs met. The client's needs are met when they're working with someone who has the knowledge and skills to help them produce their desired result. You win when you're working with a client who values your skill set and is willing to pay you what you're worth. If a potential client is not willing to pay your fees, then they do not value you in the way they claim. Although their words say one thing, their actions demonstrate how much real value they place on the work.

It's a harsh reality to face, but when we take on work with people that undervalue us, we don't get as excited about the work we're doing. So we put off the work we aren't excited about doing, and then we dread or, even worse, grow resentful about having to perform for well below our worth. Ultimately, the work we produce for this client will likely be less than our most creative. In fact, even we ourselves tend to not be thrilled with the result, because we didn't put the time into it that we would have if we had been paid our full value.

This is all said so that you can see that creating a client relationship that isn't a win-win doesn't benefit anyone. The last thing I want is for you to get to this point and fall back into **The Loop** by doing a bunch of work you don't like because you believe it's what you should do to get started. So just ignore those who will tell you that as an entrepreneur, you'd better say yes to everything because "you never know, blah blah blah." Absolutely not. Don't risk walking back into **The Loop**. You need to stay true to what you've worked so hard to create and take only those offers that will serve both you and the client. Remember, every time you say yes to something, you are

> EVERY TIME YOU SAY YES TO SOMETHING, YOU ARE SAYING NO TO SOMETHING ELSE, WHETHER YOU'RE AWARE OF IT OR NOT.

saying no to something else, whether you're aware of it or not. Consider this next time you're presented with an opportunity you know isn't a fantastic fit for you and your company.

You Can Sell—Don't Believe the Hype

We've talked about it being time to put yourself out there, and this inevitably means it's time to sell your product or services. Maybe you're immediately now saying to yourself, "Oh, but I can't sell, especially when I have to sell myself!" You can sell. Trust me. We need to challenge your idea of what it means to sell. You sell your idea, product, or capability by telling people what you believe. You sell it by sharing your why.

You see, people are drawn to those who believe what they believe themselves. And those are the people you want. Let's consider the broader perspective here. Once you have defined your market and know who your audience is, you are attached only to sharing with your audience what it is that you believe. You are no longer attached to the outcome of the sale. You're simply attached to effectively sharing with your audience that you have a solution to their problems. That means you do not need to convince or persuade anyone who doesn't believe what you believe to change their mind. I think that people's fear of sales stems from the idea that they need to be the world's greatest convincer, winning people over to their side as if they're playing a game of Red Rover the way we did as kids. All you need to do is sift and sort.

Think of it as akin to a waitress in a diner who walks along the aisle between the booths and tables pouring coffee. She isn't attached to whether or not people like coffee. She's just doing her job, walking down the aisle, saying, "Would you like coffee?" And if someone says no, she doesn't sit down at their booth and try to convince them to come over to her side and become a coffee lover. "Oh, but this is my coffee that I brewed. It's amazing. Let me tell you about the beans, which are from Colombia!" and so on. No, she's sifting and sorting through people and allowing them to self-identify. She's just offering the product she has and allowing them to tell her whether they have a need for what she's offering.

Too many people get lost in the sale. They're going on and on about the details of the product or service—"Let me tell you, this is great artistry. My technique isn't the same as anyone else's because … yada, yada." Your job is not to convince people or change anyone's mind, so take a deep breath! Your job is just to shift and sort through people, allowing them to go where they please. You're just digging through to figure out which of the people out there are your people. If a person tells you with their rejection or disinterest that they don't believe what you believe, you can just move on. That person doesn't value your artwork or your counseling or whatever product or service you provide in the same way you know your potential clients do. It's almost as if you put them to the left if they say no and to the right if they say yes. And if they imply that they believe in or feel passionately about what you're selling, then you take the next step. Only then do you dig deeper and begin to ask questions about their desires and their needs so that you can offer to meet their needs through your company. It's never about us. It is always about them—your customer.

You can move on and be grateful for the no, because that means you are closer to someone who *does* believe what you do. Now you don't have to waste your time trying to convince someone who doesn't. If you can switch your mind-set to believing all you have to do is offer, you won't waste as much of your time and energy. You can be just like the waitress in the diner who simply moves on to the next and the next and the next. Your job is merely to present the product, service, or art. It's not to sell it to someone who doesn't want it.

The customer isn't the only one who gets to walk away from the relationship. Don't be afraid of telling someone you're not a fit for them, even if it means losing a sale. Whether it's a painting or a jacket or your consulting services, your desire to create a win-win client relationship will be something they'll share with others often. You will get more long-term benefit out of that than you would out of a single client who quits working with you quickly because they realize you weren't the right fit.

Don't Deplete Your Own Potential

We often get so caught up with either the excitement or the stress of our careers that we overcommit in a desire to try to be all things to all people. One thing I learned along the way is that everything on my plate got there because I said yes to it. I'm the only person to blame if I have more than I can handle or if I've accepted a project for less than the intrinsic value of what I had to offer. This results in a feeling of emptiness that is entirely avoidable if you're aware of the pattern.

Let's say I give you a gift, a beautiful cut-crystal glass filled to the brim with water. As potential clients come to you, you convince yourself to take some who don't necessarily believe what you believe. Maybe they fall in the middle, between the no and the yes. You attempt to convince them to believe what you do, so you give some of your expertise away to them for free. This is like you pouring a little water out of your glass, believing that sharing what you have, despite the fact that it takes away from you, will benefit everyone. Maybe you decide that if you gave away a couple pieces of your artwork, or if you lowered your price for consulting, that would win you more business because you're being so generous. Bit by bit, you're emptying your glass and giving away what you have with nothing (or very little) in return.

You're pouring more and more of yourself out in the belief that if you give to others, even in a way that is taking away from yourself, you will gain, and so will they. But that's not how it works. That doesn't convert customers, convince anyone of your expertise, or make people admire your wealth of knowledge. All it does is empty your glass without refilling it, leaving you standing there with an empty glass, wondering why your business isn't thriving.

But what if you stay strong and pour into your glass by continuing to increase your knowledge, continuing to perfect your craft, sticking to your price points, and not compromising on the level of service you provide despite others asking you to? What if you stick to your guns and remain willing to serve a small market of people until the word spreads that you provide this excellent benefit? What if you always got to feel you're getting paid what you're worth without compromising? Those actions mean you're staying strong and sturdy. You're pouring into you. And if you continue to do so, your glass will overflow. The water will still reach your customers, but in an entirely different way. Both ways give water (a.k.a., your product or service) to your customers, but staying strong and letting it overflow to them is a way of giving to them that doesn't require you to suffer. You will instead be giving to your clients from a fuller, more abundant place, which benefits both of you. Both parties win. This is the type of business relationship that will lead to lasting success.

Make the Most of Your Middle Steps

Okay, let's say you've kick-started your new career, but you haven't yet made any concrete moves to get clients. Where do you go from here? By the time you have finished this book, you should have plenty of ideas regarding possible actions, but I want to share two things I did that proved to be significantly helpful in the end.

Use being *new* to your advantage. Being new to your position or as an entrepreneur is detrimental only if you believe it is. You don't need to present anyone with a detailed timeline of your career. There is often no need for you to mention how long you've been in business. Whether you are transitioning from one career or position to the next or just beginning to develop your own enterprise, you don't need to qualify yourself. We, as women, tend to feel the need to present a long explanation of our expertise or try to explain how much we know simply because our business is new. Resist that impulse. This business may be new, but you aren't!

I've discovered a shocking secret. Are you ready? No one is overly concerned about your credentials or how long you have been in business, unless you make it an issue by bringing it up. You're standing on the shoulders of the successes you've already had. You didn't lose that expertise when you made a change, so you don't have to prove anything to anyone. Even when my company was only a month old, I focused on the service I knew I could provide, the results my clients would achieve, and how I would be able to help them in a big way. That's what people really want to know about you. I knew I was going to give my clients my all, whether I had been in business for a month or a hundred months. Don't get hung up—too many people do and make it a stumbling block on their way to their destination. Push the idea that you are new to what you're doing out of your mind, and lead with how you'll serve.

Next, I got the word out on a one-to-one basis. I made a list of everyone I knew, and I mean *everyone*, not just those I thought might want to do business with me, using the FRANK tool I mentioned earlier. I sorted through that list to decide on ten people to meet with to get started. I was meeting with them simply to leave them with a good impression of me in my new role. I selected the ten people I knew had the biggest potential of making an impact on my business.

Here's the secret: I said little at these meetings other than to ask questions about them. When you ask a person about their life and what they believe, they will ultimately ask about yours in return. I didn't put a lot of pressure on the conversations. I let them flow organically, and eventually the person always asked questions about me as well. I could then respond and accomplish whatever my intention was for that meeting.

My goals for these meetings were to show up energetically and leave them with a positive feeling about both my work and me. People usually never remember what you say; they simply remember how you made them feel. I typically asked them for their views on the needs of the market, how they foresaw the future developing, and so on. I wasn't being pushy or overwhelming or fearful that I had nothing to bring to the conversation. It wasn't about me, after all. It was about learning from them and leaving them with a good impression of my company and me. The way to accomplish that is to encourage people to speak about themselves. Often the meetings would result in their introducing me to someone else or sending an email about my business to anyone they thought would benefit from my services. Some took action after our meeting, and some didn't. That's normal. But from those who did, I ended up in additional meetings with people I had never met before. One of these new contacts eventually recommended me to one of their friends at a cocktail party as a possible solution to their friend's need, and that third person hired me. That's the crazy spiderweb created when you take action and get started.

You know what? I never even got through all ten meetings I intended to have before I had enough leads and action steps to take to create new business, and I believe that if you do this and do it in the right way, you won't get through ten either. The spiderweb will already be developing, and you'll be following each direction that has spun off from your efforts.

Think of these efforts as an investment of time that's creating your future. Therefore, patience is a virtue during this stage, but so is action. I think this initial growth period is like the growth of a bamboo tree. I heard a long time ago that when you plant bamboo, it takes six years for the tree to burst out of the ground. You must keep watering it day after day, even though you can't see anything happening on the surface, but roots are forming and growing underground. It takes so long for it to break out of the ground because it's building roots that will make it strong enough to survive anything. Therefore, keep in mind that just because you can't see the results immediately doesn't mean progress isn't being made toward the growth you desire.

Be flexible, and don't be afraid to experiment. I did a lot of that in my first year, and I allowed my intuition to guide me as to whether I wanted to continue in that area long term. Remember, you are still designing your career as you go along. So be clear on your intention but fluid on how it all comes together. When you know where you're headed, you can try this route or that one. And if you end up saying, "Meh, this doesn't feel good," it's no big deal. You shift your attention from there and look in another direction. You are on the lookout for win-win situations, which are those in which you get paid your value while the client, in return, gets the best version of you because you're excited about the work you're doing. When you aren't getting paid your value but still have to show up, that's the win-lose scenario we don't want to create.

Don't Stop Stepping Forward

Never stop slowly but surely taking action to advance your business while continually evaluating your goals. It's easy to find yourself growing apprehensive, feeling like not enough is happening or even complacent at having accomplished quite a bit, especially during your first year or so in business. That could result in your thinking, *Okay, that's enough for now. I think I'll just sit back and see if what I've done is going to pay off.* But that might be the worst thing you can do. If you ever feel that way, go back and read chapter 4, and rev up your momentum. That doesn't mean you need to work at rocket speed. You simply want to stay strong and keep moving forward—after all, you're taking a giant step the majority of people dissatisfied in their careers never manage to take.

An example of someone who never stopped stepping forward is a woman I recently coached in the banking industry. She had what others judged as the perfect career arc, with a prestigious, high-level, high-six-figure position in banking. She wasn't having any bathroom floor moments, because she wasn't miserable. But over time, she had become aware that her Rock Middle simply consisted of her feeling that she deeply wanted to do something else. The most fulfilling side of her banking career was mentoring younger people as they began their careers—she had always felt **The Tug** toward helping them. Now she decided she wanted to make a greater impact by coaching and speaking to brand-new young professionals as they came out of college.

She was troubled by seeing so many people passing through the banking world and being willing to settle for comfort-zone mediocrity, going from bank to bank, making one lateral move after another. But they never took on any extra work or studied to develop themselves and their leadership skills. They never seemed willing to push themselves and take the next steps to go from being middle managers to executives. That's where she found her passion, in wanting people coming out of college to know that if they would commit to a higher level of personal development in their own careers, nothing would stop them from continuing to rise.

Her mission is to catch them early, before or just after they graduate, to help them believe in themselves and initiate them in the mind-set it takes to approach the corporate world, and the entire working world in general, in the right way. As soon as I heard what she wanted, I thought how much I wished she had been around doing what she wanted to when I was coming out of college without a clue about how to dream big. That, to me, is one of the secrets of success: remaining a lifelong learner and simply seeking a greater understanding of yourself. When you go out into the business world that way, you go out believing you can find success, not by pushing yourself relentlessly, but by becoming your best self.

Once she knew her *why*—to help young people love their careers and become the people they were meant to be—she could roughly define her *how* (by envisioning herself speaking at colleges and universities in addition to providing one-on-one coaching). And once she had that nailed down, she could take her first steps to move ahead. These were steps she could take without giving up her job or exhausting herself, because they had no deadlines. First, she could make a list of schools she would like to visit, moving out in concentric circles from her base and highlighting those where she had contacts or could most easily make them. Then, she had to develop her own curriculum. She decided on three topics she could address in front of students and graduates. These weren't set in stone. She didn't fear making a mistake, because she knew her business would evolve as she learned the needs of her market. She could only learn from getting into action. That's exactly what she did, all the way to the fulfillment she had once only imagined.

How to Keep Going When Your Trust Tapers

We all have our ups and downs, especially when we're daring to strike out on our path and go off in search of our dream instead of society's version of success. How can you keep yourself from deciding your new direction was a bad decision and that you should back off and retreat to safety? Try to remember a few of the core lessons we've discussed that will help you.

Stick with facts, not feelings. When you feel low and self-doubt creeps in, when a feeling strikes you or a discouraging belief obsesses you, stop and ask yourself if it's 100 percent true. Remind yourself that it is a fact that growth is uncomfortable but will lead to a place of fulfillment and abundance.

Approach any setbacks with curiosity. We tend to fall into snap judgments and knee-jerk reactions. Just think how much of social media is based on this trait! If someone rejects us by not wanting to work or collaborate with us, our unconscious decision is to treat it as a problem or a failure. The real problem is that, when we look at it that way, we tend to stop. Refashion your thinking so you can look at any perceived setback as laying the ground for something better. Approaching things with curiosity and wonder versus fear and frustration is a choice you can make that will buoy you up and encourage you to keep going to see where whatever happened will lead you. Ask yourself, "I wonder how this is coming together for my betterment rather than for my detriment?"

Scratch the either/or paradigm. This is not only a mode of thinking you don't need, it's a hindrance rather than a help. Always. Remember, you don't want your pendulum swinging back and forth between zero and ten. That will run you ragged. Say no to anything that doesn't fall into the category of "Hell, yes!" as that won't fill your crystal glass. Strive to lead your life in the four-five-six zone.

Break away from excuses. Define the good habits that are your building blocks now, and ignore the limiting beliefs that were your excuses in the past.

The next step is the only one you need to take. If you look too far ahead, you can feel overwhelmed. Know your goals and long-term vision, but climb the staircase to your dream one step at a time.

You don't need to reinvent yourself to put these suggestions into action. In fact, I hope you've already gotten started on some of them. You have everything you need within you right now to reach your dream. You just need to believe that you do, and you'll be well ahead of most people. I'm confident that you have it inside you and you wouldn't have been on this journey to get started if you weren't meant for more.

YOUR ROCK MIDDLE REMINDER:

To make progress, you need to commit to only two things: belief in your own value and putting one foot in front of the other.

GO BIG, GO BOLD!

Release the past, enjoy the present, and have faith in the future.

—GABBY BERNSTEIN

You have read my story and the stories of other women who got unstuck and discovered their true callings, careers that lay dormant inside them for years. I hope these stories inspired you and showed you how other people kept taking steps on their continuous journey and ultimately reached freedom and fulfillment. If they can do it, you can too. There's nothing unique about them. As I said, they were just willing to walk through the gap between their comfort zone and where the magic happens. They dared to trudge through the unknown and a bit of personal growth to find out the habits, patterns, and beliefs that were holding them back from their greatest potential. I hope their stories will continue to feed your imagination and decision-making processes as you plan your journey. I am happy to add that none of them has ever regretted taking themselves out of **The Loop**.

The road ahead doesn't have to be hard or long. Don't fall into the trap of hesitating to take a step that could result in quick advancement. For years, I've seen people who are unwilling to move forward—to take their first step. They aren't willing to take that chance, sometimes out of fear and lack of confidence, but often simply because they believe the road to success has to be a long, hard, upward slog. The road to success lies in not thinking that way.

The real estate agent/comic got up the nerve to enter a comedy competition against seasoned pros. Even though she had officially been in the business only a short time, she fine-tuned her routines and put herself out there to be judged in an elimination competition. She put herself on the line and risked rejection, and she won. It doesn't have to take a lifetime to get where you want to go. It can happen in the blink of an eye if you're willing to take a risk.

> IT DOESN'T HAVE TO TAKE A LIFETIME TO GET WHERE YOU WANT TO GO. IT CAN HAPPEN IN THE BLINK OF AN EYE IF YOU'RE WILLING TO TAKE A RISK.

Remember the printing company executive who wanted to be an artist? He positioned himself to find commissions painting large landscapes, with an eye to getting established with corporate and construction clients. Instead of keeping his circle of influence small and trying to get started bit by bit, he went big. Rather than try to act small, which can hold out to the world that you and your dream are small, he planned a giant launch party for his new company. Though he had been an artist for a long time, this was the first time he presented himself to the world as an established and successful artist looking for collaborations, commissions, and future projects. Taking one step at a time doesn't mean any of those steps has to be a small one.

Being your boldest self doesn't have to be expensive either. It's more a state of mind and a willingness to put yourself out there for everyone to see you show off what you do with confidence and joy, whether as a comic, an artist, or anything else. The saleswoman who wanted to be an art consultant? She made a low-cost but bold move in presenting herself to the public via Instagram, opening an account in her company name and hiring a photographer to take photos that showed her skills in choosing and displaying art. She was scared to death of what others might say and think, but she trusted her intuition. Don't forget that if you're still in your comfort zone, it means you haven't gone far enough. Having concerns and butterflies in your stomach is a good thing.

The result was that she immediately got messages on Instagram that developed into being hired for projects throughout two states. It doesn't have to take forever to get where you want to go. It can happen overnight, or it can take a bit of time, but as long as you keep your enthusiasm high and your steps progressive, you will get there.

While an Instagram account might not sound like a big deal to you, it was to her, and it took a lot emotionally for her to put herself out there in that way. Doing something like that is a symbolic gesture that shows the world for the first time who you really want to be, and that *is* a big deal. She didn't hold herself back, minimize herself in an effort to avoid being criticized, or choose the safer path.

The artist who turned down the "dream" project? Her business has done spectacularly well. She hit the typical fears and challenges we all face when we make changes. But she continued to expand. In fact, after she got her biggest commission on the heels of turning down that project, her business expanded so quickly, it made my head spin. After your first initial expansion, you need to be willing— as she was—to go on to do the next expansion of who you are in order to get to the full level of where you're meant to be. She's facing each expansion with energy and excitement, and her business is benefiting each time she does.

The public relations firm owner who wanted to start an online educational program to teach other businesses how to handle their own PR found she had much of what she needed just by leaning into her own expertise, her translatable skills. She had, from her PR business, many of the tools and contacts needed to create this new entity, and she leveraged them. Once she got past her own hesitation and vulnerability, she went bold quickly. She realized how many of the tools her old company had created for clients over the years could be refashioned for the new company, and that's what she did. She mined her own assets, looking at them in a new way as the foundation of her new venture.

And the client you learned of most recently, the senior banking executive with the desire to help young people streamline and expand their career goals, made her first bold step by contacting and meeting with the college recruiters on her list. She's now in the process of launching her website and creating a podcast to share her leadership knowledge and career wisdom with a much wider audience.

> I BELIEVE THAT EVERYTHING YOU HAVE EVER WANTED IS BEING HELD IN DIVINE TRUST FOR YOU. YOU TRULY CAN'T MESS IT UP. YOU CAN ONLY FAIL TO GO AFTER IT.

I hope the progress of these clients shows you that it is all possible, no matter how many times you've previously tried or failed. I believe that everything you have ever wanted is being held in divine trust for you. You truly can't mess it up. You can only fail to go after it. So don't waste another minute questioning your dream or waiting for the right moment.

Are You Prepared to Be Bold?

If you have learned something, been inspired, or gotten motivated by my story and the others I have shared, I have accomplished all I set out to, and I thank you for sharing the journey with me. Each of us experienced Rock Middle in our own way; some of us hit it with a moderate impact, and some hit it hard (I'm raising my hand here). We all forged ahead and created our new path in the wheat field—we'd had it with the well-worn path that had led us only to **The Loop** every time.

We didn't find the success of being who we were meant to be and doing what we had a passion for by dumb luck. We pulled ourselves up, and we faced the demons that had been keeping us from realizing our true potential. You can do it too. You just need to commit to BE BOLDER and go big with unrestrained enthusiasm. I break it down this way:

B *Begin to dream again.* Beginning to dream again frees you from the confines of your current career or the skill set you now have and income you might be able to generate so you can move into the future from a wide-open, wondrous place, knowing what being your best self might look like.

E *Envision your new future.* Once you've thrown everything on the table and picked out the pieces and parts that will work for your burgeoning self, envision yourself in five or ten years having achieved your dream. Who are you, and what have you done?

B *Beware of blind spots.* Do a gut check to be honest about what stopped you from getting to your dream in the past. What has kept you in **The Loop**? What assumptions have you made about yourself that have kept you from looking outside your current career or position? These are your blind spots, and recognizing them is your moment of truth.

O *Overcome obstacles.* Assumptions about your own abilities and limited thinking about the existence of opportunities can undermine your drive to change. This thinking concerns generalizations that can seem like roadblocks, such as "men can't be artists," "you don't know enough to get started," and the general but mistaken hope-killer, "So and so has done this before." But these obstacles are never true barriers to your success. And outside of societal assumptions, most of them aren't genuine obstacles at all—they're just your old habits, patterns, and beliefs.

L *Look around at social proof.* Never let yourself forget that there are people out there doing something similar to what you want to do, doing it with less education and less experience than you have right now. When you're thinking you can't do what you want, look for opportunities to prove yourself wrong, not right.

D *Design it by reverse engineering from your goal.* It's easy to defeat yourself when you start from the beginning, because the things that come to mind often have nothing to do with achieving your ultimate goal. If you start with "These are the four things I do, and here are the price ranges" rather than your ultimate goal, you're working in the dark and will likely waste time on actions that don't move you ahead. Don't throw spaghetti on the wall. Start with the end, then make a list of the goals that will help you reach that final destination. Then list the actions that will help you make each goal happen.

E *Evaluate and sell it.* You need to believe in your new future because the first and most important person you have to sell it to is yourself. When you believe in it with your whole body and soul and believe in the value you add to others, nothing can stop you. After that, you can just follow the lead of that waitress pouring coffee. You need not worry about the outcome; just start offering what you have to others.

R *Run with it by taking the next step.* Get into action. You don't have to overcome every obstacle or take more than one step today. Don't waste time being or feeling overwhelmed. Just keep moving, focusing on the steps that propel you forward and motivating yourself never to give up on your dream or your skills. One step a day leads up to 365 steps a year—more than enough to realize whatever your ambition may be.

Do all this, and you won't think about giving up on your dream. Nor will you need to. I promise that you will have succeeded in realizing your dream. You're already on the way, because you have seen that success isn't how things look on the outside, that it doesn't revolve around a title or a career. Success is a feeling of fulfillment on the inside. It's getting home at the end of the day and feeling the deepest satisfaction in having spent your time aligned with your greatest vision for your life and career. Most people would say that the careers I had before I really started chasing my dream were much more within the societal definition of success. But I feel more successful now than I ever have in my life, because I'm doing something I love and believe in. After all, I'm helping other people do things that they love and believe in too, while getting to be my joyful, authentic self every single day. I'm excited for that success to be yours, too.

GET OUT OF ROCK MIDDLE STARTING TODAY!

Visit **https://sallieholder.com** to get the resources you need to get started creating the future you know you're capable of having.

FREE RESOURCES

- Subscribe to the Hitting Rock Middle Podcast available on iTunes, Spotify, & more.

- Subscribe to Sallie's weekly newsletter giving you top tips for achieving your goals

GETTING OUT OF ROCK MIDDLE E-COURSE

Don't just stop with this book. Now is the time to take action and create your plan for getting out of "Rock Middle." If you're the person who hopes they can achieve more with their life – you're actively seeking fulfillment and success, not just one or the other - and you are willing to challenge the habits, patterns and beliefs holding you back, then you're the perfect person to take this E-Course.

This 10-module online learning course will take you step by step through the BE BOLDER framework. It will help you transform your life and career into one you're excited to get to live. You'll learn to eliminate the use of negative self-talk; the need to hustle; perfectionism tendencies that stop you; and thinking you need to be an expert before you get started. You'll start protecting your energy; living in a state of curiosity; and holding yourself accountable. When you finish this course, you'll walk away with the entire roadmap of how to achieve the dreams you've longed to make a reality.

SPEAKING ENGAGEMENTS

Give your audience the opportunity to be inspired to get out of "Rock Middle" too. Sallie will bring her dynamic, engaging personality to light up your audience. She's a nationally recognized public speaker who has trained employees for many of the companies on the Fortune 100 list. See more information about several of Sallie's speeches at https://sallieholder.com/speaking/. Reach out to have Sallie customize a speech to your audience.

COACHING

Sallie offers both Group Coaching & One to One Private Business Coaching. Information about both can be found on her website. Group Coaching sessions are offered intermittently throughout the year. One to one coaching is offered on a first come, first serve basis. To inquire about either, reach out to admin@sallieholder.com.